About the Author

At age of four, Vera Hemsley was asked to draw a picture of what she wanted to be when she grew up. Her match-stick image of a woman with a red cross on her cap and apron was clear for everyone to see.

This delightful memoir follows Vera's journey into nursing, recounting some of her most memorable anecdotes along the way. From sneaking out of the Nurse's Home during training, to the pranks played by hospital staff, and the colourful characters on a district nurse's round – Vera tells it all!

Sometimes touching, yet humorous throughout *Don't Panic! It's only the Nurse* gives a personal insight into a unique career. There is something to make every reader smile along the way.

Don't Panic! It's Only the Nurse

Vera Hemsley

Don't Panic! It's Only the Nurse

Olympia Publishers
London

www.olympiapublishers.com
OLYMPIA PAPERBACK EDITION

A CIP catalogue record for this title is
available from the British Library.

ISBN: 978-1-78830-546-4

This is a work of creative nonfiction. The events are portrayed to the
best of the author's memory. While all the stories in this book are
true, some names and identifying details have been changed to
protect the privacy of the people involved.

First Published in 2020
Olympia Publishers
Tallis House
2 Tallis Street
London
EC4Y 0AB

Printed in Great Britain

Dedication

I would like to dedicate this book to the wonderful oncology team who not only saved my life, but were passionate in all they did, and still do in the East Lancashire NHS.

Consultant Dr Apell and all her team.
My MacMillan nurse, Paul McKenna.

Acknowledgements

A big 'Thanks' to all the friends who supported me in the writing of this book.
Carole, Kay, Lynda, Danielle and especially Beryl who helped make this possible.
And to the numerous people whose encouragement has meant so much.

PREFACE

This book is a reflection of many years of working with people, and of caring for them. I could easily recall many sad stories, which would give a very different slant to what has been written.

However, I also enjoy humour and fun, and believe the saying 'laugh and the world laughs with you, weep and you weep alone'.

This book is more about the individual anecdotes during my thirty odd years of nursing, and afterwards. All are true accounts of my experiences. The short stories within these pages reflect my sense of humour. They are designed for easy reading, and an insight into how I managed to make it through to retirement, and still be able to laugh out loud at the memories.

Part One

IMPORTANT INSTRUCTIONS

Have you ever been in a situation where you wanted to laugh uncontrollably, but it was inappropriate?

The following served me well during my nursing career and beyond. I still use it to this day.

Nurses' Facial Expression

I need to explain to the reader about this term. It is adaptable to most walks of life, and there are still situations which warrant this default expression. It became my fail-safe mechanism for dealing with the many adventures that have been fondly brought back to life in this little book.

Nurses' Facial Expression (NFE)

The Technique

1. Do not show any emotion other than sympathy.
2. Ensure that your face does not contort into laughter.
3. Try not to use direct eye contact until your face is under control.
4. Allow your eyes to widen but keep your gaze straight.
5. Finally, when overwhelmed with the situation, allow the nostrils to gently flare, this being the only clue that your deepest wish is to roll about in hysterical laughter.

I quickly became aware that I needed to cultivate my NFE. I did in fact, manage to do this early on; I still use it when I come across situations which would send me into fits of laughter. For anyone dealing with the general public, and finding themselves in a hilarious situation which warrants a straight face DO try this at home with the following list of 'one-liners' which caught me off guard.

For future reference, this will be known as NFE.

THE ONE-LINERS:

Medication

1. Apply locally (cream/ointment)
   Patient's comment: "Won't be able to go out much, my family live ten miles away." (Patient thought he had to stay near his home to apply it.)

2. Aminophylene suppositories (rectal medication to help breathing)
   Very nasal comment from patient: "These suppositories don't half hurt, the plastic makes my nose sore."

3. Salbutamol Inhaler.
   "Oh nurse, it doesn't work, I can't get it onto my teaspoon."

Anatomy

4. "Oh Nurse, my lungs are really hurting." (Rubbing both groins.)

5. "I have a Colostofer you know." (Colostomy – pretty close.)

6. "I'm Diabolic, it runs in the family." (Diabetic)

Medical problem (Think deeply about this one)

7. "Doctor, I need your help; I can only ejaculate to a distance of six feet."

FIRST STEPS

Having left the army, I knew that nursing was still in my blood and that it was now time to complete my lifelong desire. In the 1970s, recruitment and training was very different than it is today. The first step was to attend an interview, which mainly seemed to assess whether my motives and abilities would match the criteria for training.

I chose to train in Leicester, and so attended an interview at The Charles Frears School of Nursing. In those days there were two types of nurse training for those who were happy doing bedside nursing State Enrolled Nurse.

If you had gained any paper qualifications i.e. GCEs etc., you were guided onto the path of training for three years, to become a State Registered Nurse.

I found myself sitting in the waiting area at the School of Nursing, feeling very nervous and wondering if I had made the right decision (my parents still thought it was a foolish move). At last my turn came, and I was ushered into an office, where three very official looking people were waiting. They introduced themselves as Tutor, Matron, and Vicar. The tutor's role was to ascertain if I had the brains to do the studying; The matron was to assess my attitudes and behaviours; the vicar was there to assess if my motives were genuine, and in the interests of the patients I was to care for. I returned home to anxiously await the results of my interview. A fortnight later I received my acceptance letter, and I was allocated to the next intake of students, to become known as 'The January '76 Set.'

The Home Sister

In those days it was the norm to live in the Nurses' Home while training. The accommodation was a small bedsit type room, with a communal kitchen for the use of the students. Mostly we were expected to eat in the hospital canteen. However, along with the accommodation came the Home Sister, who was a force to reckoned with. Her room was strategically placed so that the students had to walk past it to access the world outside. Students were forbidden to be on the loose after 9 p.m. The Home Sister ensured that we weren't.

It became an art to sneak past her room, and escape to what seemed like normality. On our days off, we were allowed to stay out a little longer, but never to return with a member of the opposite sex. I think she would have terrified any prospective boyfriends. How on earth did the Home Sister know so much about us? She knew us by name, what we were doing, where we'd come from and most of all – by our behaviours. On the few occasions that we'd escaped past her door, she would be there waiting for us on our return. Nothing I'd experienced in the army prepared me for the fear of the Home Sister!

On one occasion, I and four others decided that we would like to nip to the hospital canteen for some supper. It was past the curfew time, and we knew that the sister would be guarding our escape route.

We had discovered an external fire escape, and had worked out that we could use it to reach the canteen. It wasn't easy, but it worked, though we had quite an arduous path to follow. Our goal was a quarter of a mile away and involved more than one very slippery fire escape.

I was chosen to do the first run, and with great trepidation, was up and down various fire escapes until I was clear of the Nurses' Home. I remembered thinking, 'We've cracked it, and there IS a way out, other than past the sister's room.' And so, having found the way to the canteen, I returned to get the other four students to follow me. In those days, we were not allowed to take food out of the canteen, 'take-aways' didn't exist. We returned an hour later – around 11 p.m., having retraced our steps back to the Nurses' Home. We were all jubilant that our new mode of escape was a path to freedom.

NOT SO!

As we quietly re-entered the home via the fire escape, there, in all her glory, was the woman who terrified us the most! Even scarier was the fact that we had kept her up, and she was clad in night attire; hair in rollers and held in place with a hairnet. Her dressing gown was tied tightly around her waist, and she had some rather large slippers on her feet. Our joy and excitement at finding an escape route immediately evaporated. She didn't have to speak, her every pore exuded her wrath. She intently looked at each of us, stood back and indicated we return to our rooms.

Only four words passed her lips:
"I'll be watching you!"

Into the Fray

Around that time in the '70s, changes were taking place. Matrons were being phased out and nurse managers stepping in. In those days, the nursing ranks were surrounded by discipline, position and status. No one appeared to have first names, just titles and surname.

After six weeks introduction to nursing in the school, we were allocated our first placements on the wards. Our uniforms had been issued to us during that six weeks, and comprised a white dress, white cotton belt and the student nurse paper hat. The hat indicated what stage of your training you were at: year one had one blue stripe, year two had two stripes, and the final year had three. Enrolled nurse trainees were referred to as pupils, as opposed to students and had corresponding stripes which were green.

We walked onto the ward, and it seemed endless; a Florence Nightingale ward, as they were better known. My first allocation was a medical ward, and seemed to stretch 'as far as the eye could see'. Thirty-six beds on the main ward, and another eight on the balcony. I was mesmerised, there were real patients in the beds. Some had tubes and drips and all sorts trailing from them. Further down, I could see patients sitting next to their beds. The nurses changed the sheets and made them up again with the infamous 'hospital corners'. One of my first most memorable thoughts was, 'I am getting paid money to help these people'. It was a very scary time, and we were here to learn. And so it began.

A Long Stand

It was almost traditional in those early days for the new student nurse to go through many forms of pranks, usually instigated by the qualified nurses. I am aware now that it amused the staff to send the unsuspecting trainee on various errands.

One of the most common 'errands' was to say quite seriously to the first year student, 'please go to the theatre for a long stand', (the learner assuming it was an intra-venous drip stand), as there was a shortage on the ward. Always eager to please, the student nurse would 'hot foot' to theatre, where the request for a long stand was made. Of course, there was never any disappointment. The theatre sister would ask which ward had requested the long stand, making a mental guess of whom the joker was likely to be. Usually, the student was asked to stand somewhere in the theatre, where they wouldn't have to move much, and were out of the way. Of course the learner was always in awe and respectful of the ranks above her. And so, there she stood in the corner, waiting for the long stand to appear. The surgeon hid behind his mask but there remained a slight twinkle of humour in his eyes, fully knowing what was going on. The remainder of the staff went about their work and the student, waiting, did not dare to remind anyone about the request for a 'long stand'.

Usually, half an hour or so later, the timid nurse was told she could return to her ward. Perplexed and confused, the inevitable question arrived:

"But where is the long stand I've been sent for?"

The inevitable reply being, "You have just had a long stand, have you not?"

The poor student, a little red around the gills, and somewhat flustered, would return to her ward empty handed.

A similar prank involved the student being asked to go for a pair of Fallopian Tubes.

She would return to the ward, having had a rather speedy anatomy lesson by one of the theatre staff.

Hot Stool Specimen

It was quite normal for the students to take various specimens to the laboratory because the results were needed quickly and the specimens were often obtained between the normal collection times.

It didn't seem unusual to me, to be asked to transport a 'hot stool specimen' to the laboratory. Having little knowledge at that point of the various receptacles used for the purpose. And so, when the nurse in charge told me that I was required to take this particular specimen to the 'Path Lab' (pathology laboratory), I didn't question it. Mr Smith had just passed a motion, and I was to take the commode bucket (with lid on) through all the corridors and public areas on route to the Path Lab. I remember it being a very long walk – about half a mile. My most important task was to get there before it cooled down. Running was against the rules, so I walked as fast as I could, negotiating twists and turns and of course, trying to avoid bumping into the general public as they innocently went about their business.

I remember seeing the signs announcing Pathology, and an arrow to direct me to it. As I reached my destination I quickly felt the side of the commode bucket, hoping that my specimen was still warm enough. As I entered the Path Lab, the receptionist simply asked, "WHAT IS THAT?"

At the time it seemed obvious to me what it was, and so I placed it on the counter and proudly replied that it was a hot stool specimen and it was still warm.

There was something in her demeanour that didn't feel right to me. She appeared to be perplexed, which then turned to a dawning of what was going on. With fire in her eyes, she informed me that ALL specimens are placed in the required receptacles and labelled appropriately with the patient's details. A commode bucket was NOT one of those containers. At that point, she instructed me to inform the nurse in charge to adhere to the rules, and use the specimen pots as directed. To say the least, I was crestfallen. Not only that, I had to return the not-so-hot stool specimen back to the ward.

As I entered the ward, the nurse who had sent me on the errand knowing full well what the outcome would be, looked appropriately surprised, not understanding why the Path Lab refused to accept the now cold stool specimen. I glanced around; heads were suddenly buried in other activities, appearing not to be aware of the prank. However, as I passed the sister's office later, there was laughter and frivolity as my escapade was discussed at length! As I look back, I know that nowadays any such ideas would never come to fruition, and very likely disciplinary action would follow.

Making Tents

It was part of our training to experience night time nursing. Reduced staff meant that you worked 'closer' as a team. Usually there would be two trained staff, two students and a nursing auxiliary (now known as health care assistants).

Working eight nights on and six off was quite hard, especially since we worked eleven hour shifts. It was literally bed and work. The first hours were spent helping patients to bed, and doing 'the back-round'. This comprised of a trolley, a bar of soap, towels, spare sheets, bedpans, and urinals. The bedpans were stainless steel and the urinals were made of glass.

Unlike today, where there is a named nurse for each patient, the work was task orientated. Someone was allocated to do the 'observations' – which included temperatures, pulses, and blood pressures, fondly known as 'teeps and beeps'. I trained mainly on the Florence Nightingale wards, which had forty-two beds and were usually fully occupied. It often took a couple of hours to settle patients down for the night.

The back-round, consisted of taking the trolley to each patient, offering bedpans/commodes or bottles. Each patient then had their pressure areas treated. This was done by soaping up one gloved hand and rubbing the patient's pressure areas. Elbows, heels and bums were duly treated, sheets changed if necessary, and used bedpans retrieved. By the time this task was completed, the 'teeps and beeps' had been done and the trained nurse had given out the various medications.

We started the shift at 9 p.m. and that part of the night's work was done by around 11:30 p.m. Unlike on the day shift, we would make a sneaky cuppa in the ward kitchen, usually hiding it behind the desk, in case someone came. That someone was the night sister, who visited all the wards and proceeded to escort the staff to each patient, one by one. She expected the accompanying nurse and student to know names, ages and diagnosis of all forty-two patients. I swear that woman could smell our brews at the other end of the hospital. It seemed to give her a strange form of pleasure, to ensure our drinks were stone cold by the end of her visit.

One of my night secondments was on an orthopaedic ward and, consequently, there was a variety of ages that made up the patient head count on that unit. Some were elderly who had broken a hip, some were young men who had broken bones as a result of accidents, crashes and sometimes fighting.

Of the forty-two, about thirty-two were on the main ward and a further ten on the balcony. Each patient was visited by the night sister. However, that woman was a law unto herself. There was a little twist to her visit on the orthopaedic ward. Young men, being young men had their own pastimes at night and although their broken limbs didn't work too well, other parts of their anatomy did. On many occasions, there were some activities that the men seemed to enjoy. In the night sister's words, they were 'making tents' under the sheets. Her night time ward round encompassed a slow walk down the balcony, eyes darting up and down, and focusing on the tents that had been created.

To my horror, out came her pen and, with the accuracy of a well-practiced fly swatter, she made her way down the row of men, flicking each tent in turn. The effect was immediate: the tents collapsed. The night sister, not one for showing any feelings, could be seen with a satisfied glint in her eye. The young men however, could not!

And so my training continued, and various secondments went on.

IZAL Toilet Paper

During my final year, I had the experience of being seconded to a psychiatric unit on the outskirts of Leicester. This was a very different part of my training, and nothing could ever have prepared me for what I was to learn, during those twelve weeks.

The facility was a 'lock up' ward, where patients were 'sectioned' under the Mental Health Act. This meant that they existed in almost prison like conditions. The charge nurse had the biggest bunch of keys imaginable. There was a key for every door, bedroom, office etcetera. The reasons became apparent as we discovered the nature of the mental illnesses suffered by these patients.

Safety came first, meaning that the office was a safe haven, was kept locked, and had an emergency call button and bullet proof glass in the windows. Should a patient decide to attack, refuge was sought in the office until help arrived. Some of the patients had been there for many years. One was the product of an affair between two of the patients, some years earlier. Sadly, the mental illness had been passed on and they too had become an inpatient.

The work was varied and once settled onto the ward, the students began to feel more at ease and would take part in the daily routines. One of those routines was the issuing of cigarettes after meals. Not all patients were able to afford this commodity. They managed to get their tobacco supply via other methods. Considering that many (not all) had some mental capacities, there was a culture of obtaining tobacco, via the more affluent clients. They simply collected the many cigarette butts left by others who had been issued with a supply. Methodically, and in pecking order, the less fortunate would collect the tobacco from the extinguished cigarettes found in ash trays (and many other places). The next problem was that of obtaining the roll-up papers, which seemed to be non-existent. I saw these people smoking, and wondered where their supply of papers came from.

I decided to sit down and have a chat with the clients and to observe the methods used to get the desired nicotine hit.

Connie was an old hand at it. She had been there many years and it seemed that she would remain there. Her condition was too unstable and she was ill equipped to return to the outside world. After lunch, the cigarettes were issued. Usually between two and five were given, supposedly to last until teatime. Connie remained patient whilst the others smoked away. She was top of the pecking order: when it came to butt ends, no one would dare to try jumping the queue.

She methodically went around the ash trays and retrieved enough tobacco to create a roll up. This was the moment of truth. Where did the paper come from? I watched as she made her way to the toilets, returning with the only type of toilet paper that was used by the hospital – IZAL. This paper was produced for many years and its most outstanding feature was its non-absorbency; probably many of you will remember it. IT MADE PERFECT ROLL UPS.

Now I understood how it was done. However, it did have its downside and a highly dangerous one at that. Once alight, if it wasn't rolled tightly enough, the paper would flare up, resembling a blow torch.

I cannot imagine why, considering the dangers, it was ever allowed. Connie herself had a close call; we found a badly burned vest in the laundry with her name on it. She was one of the patients who could wash herself and change her own clothes. The burn marks were glaring at us, and had destroyed much of the vest. Luckily for Connie, she only received very minor burns to her chest. She quickly recovered, but kept on smoking. After the incident she was constantly monitored by the staff, to ensure her safety.

The end of the IZAL era came during my secondment there, possibly due to that incident. It was not a popular move, but the IZAL was replaced by the type of loo paper used today. It is difficult to imagine the horror of the patients when this happened. Many tried desperately to use the new toilet tissue, to no avail. It simply smouldered and fell apart.

My time spent in the lock-up unit was quite surreal. It was a world of its own, and a dangerous one at times. For some reason, to specialise in mental health did not appeal to me! It must be said that my experience there was only a small snapshot, but my leanings were towards the general nursing side and that's where I headed.

ACCIDENT AND EMERGENCY

That's no Accident!

This experience remains a very memorable six weeks; variety, surprises and literally traumas. There were more staff, but it was busy. Leicester Royal Infirmary had a large turnover of patients. As students, our roles involved some very different aspects of nursing. Only during our late second or early third year of training were we allowed to be seconded there. Many times we were 'runners', setting up equipment for doctors and qualified staff.

A Stitch in Time

There were occasional quieter times, and the nurse in charge would gather students in a cubicle to learn the art of suturing wounds. We initially used oranges to practice our techniques, until it was almost perfected.

Saturday nights have always been busy in A&E, and the usual influx of patients consisted of some very drunken young men. Some had been fighting, some had fallen down, and some had been injured by glass beer bottles. Each one was assessed by the medical team and categorised according to the injury. Many of them were dirty, had been incontinent and some were covered in blood and vomit. The particularly messed up patients who needed only a stitch or two were taken to the forecourt and hosed down. The clothing was put in a bin bag and a theatre gown replaced the missing items. To further our training, the Department Sister would assess wounds, and clear the surrounding skin of debris or hair.

Once this had been done (the drunk was totally unaware of what was going on) we, the students, had our chance to improve our suturing skills. Local anaesthetic wasn't always necessary, as booze had done the job. Both student doctors and student nurses were then able to improve their art of stitching!

The Fruit Bowl

I still remember the guy who was called through to be seen by a doctor. We tended to call the more ambulant clients 'the walking wounded'. On this occasion, his walk seemed somewhat laboured, and he was definitely uncomfortable.

In those days, there wasn't a triage nurse; patients were ushered into a cubicle where a nurse took a brief history. It was pretty straight forward to record the details, name address, GP, and a 'potted history' of the injury.

A man in his late twenties walked in with some discomfort. He was quite nervous and ill at ease. This of course was normal and I reassured him that he would be taken care of and that we could sort out his condition/injury.

As I began to take the history of his problem, he became more and more nervous but, having had two years training, I felt my reassuring manner would help. I guessed that something quite personal was worrying him, so I reassured him that nothing would shock us, or indeed, upset me.

He finally muttered that he had slipped on the fruit bowl in his home. I secretly glanced at every part of his body that I could see but there was nothing No cuts, no blood, nothing, yet he still looked to be in a lot of discomfort.

"Errrrm, I slipped as I stepped over the fruit bowl, and an orange got stuck in my back passage." (Whaaaaat?)

I must add my NFE, which came to serve me well in the future years, hadn't quite reached perfection at that time in my career.

I rapidly created an excuse to leave the cubicle, until I had composed myself. My imagination ran riot. Who walks over a fruit bowl with no trousers on? Why was it on the floor, and how on earth did the orange reach its destination? Of course, after going through the scenario in my head, there was only one explanation. Luckily, I managed to pass the case to an unsuspecting junior doctor, who then continued taking the medical history. The orange was duly extracted without the need for an operation.

Joined at the Hip

As with most A&E departments, even in those days, the ambulance control centre would phone-in cases which needed seeing as soon as possible and a cubicle would be prepared.

I remember once, in the early hours of the morning, we had 'the phone call' and we hastily prepared the cubicle, but were instructed that two casualties needed to share the same bed. As students, we hadn't come across this situation. We waited in the side-lines to discover the nature of their injuries. As the two patients were wheeled in on the stretcher, it became apparent why they had to be seen together. The male and female were, for want of a better word, joined at their hips!

It very occasionally happens that during sexual intercourse, the female vagina can go into spasm, locking down on the man's penis, consequently becoming inseparable.

Treatment can be speedy and effective; and after being assessed by the duty registrar, the female was given a muscle relaxant, which freed the man from her 'grip'. The ambulance men too, had that wonderful ability not to show any emotional reactions to their patients' plight. The only clue was a furrowing of their eyebrows. ADMIRABLE.

Next Please.

On the odd occasion, we had quiet moments in the department, with only perhaps four or five patients waiting to be seen. It was such an intense type of nursing that in the quieter times we would lighten the mood. As with most waiting areas in hospitals, one of the nurses would go and shout the name of the next patient to be seen.

We were quite creative behind the scenes and would come up with some fictitious names to call out. Wishing to practise my NFE, I would gather myself, wearing my best version of it, and call out a predesigned name. Most patients would look in the direction of the nurse when there was hope of being called in to be examined. Clearing my throat, and holding some 'medical notes', I would stand in view of all, and shout, "Mr Ben Dover, Mustafa Pee, Leya Down."

The patients would glance around to see who stood up. I would then mutter something about them visiting the loo, and return to the giggling pranksters behind the scenes.

QUALIFIED

Becoming A Real Nurse

The final part of our training was to take the written examinations. We had already undergone the practical assessments, which involved doing a drug round, aseptic dressing technique, and other such hands-on tests.

The written exams were a full day, involving essays on patient care followed by a multiple choice questionnaire. Waiting for the results seemed like a lifetime. A postal strike made matters worse, as we had to phone up the School of Nursing for our results.

Four of us were very close and became strong friends, each wanting the other to qualify. After contacting our tutors, we were given a phone number to call and the results of our three years of training would be given. We agreed to make the calls, but each of us would then go to our room and wait until we had all heard our fate. Eventually, we learned that three had passed, and one had failed. This took away our joy of success and for the following four months the three remaining friends went to the failed student's room to help her with her revision. Liz went on to pass her finals, and the four of us were jubilant.

The next step was to secure a job and, in those days, there

were enough jobs to employ the newly qualified staff. I was ecstatic when accepted by the staff of the very same medical ward where I had encountered the 'hot stool specimen' prank.

The next phase of my nursing had started. Our new uniforms were issued; by this time the starched aprons had disappeared and plastic disposable ones had been substituted. However, for some months, we still had the frilly hat to wear, as a mark of our status. Now we were known as staff nurses.

I spent many hours creating these frilly hats for the other newly-qualified staff. There was a definite art to their creation. It started off as a limp piece of cotton material, edged with lace. There was a knack to using the starch and the special way to fold the material to create the finished product.

I became quite skilled at it, and made 'a mint' from my colleagues, who hadn't quite got the knack. Sadly, along with the starched aprons, the hats disappeared too. Understandably, hygiene and cross infection issues were at the forefront of these changes. It was around the same time when bandages which were dutifully washed and re-used were phased out too.

Now I was part of the qualified team of nurses and became the teacher of students. It has to be said, looking from the other side of the coin, the reality of the responsibility became glaringly apparent to me. I took it very seriously and, as a staff nurse, was part of the team which held the ward together and ensured the best patient care we could offer.

Bed Rest

In the '70s, patients admitted with a heart attack were put on bed rest. Usually a cardiac monitor was in place and the patient was observed in one of the beds near to the nurses' desk, so that they could be closely watched. Bed rest meant the patient could get up to use the commode and use a urinal in bed. The urinals were made of glass, and were washed in the sluice after use. The commodes were similar to today, but perhaps a little heavier.

As with most wards, the students and pupil nurses were keen to help these dependent patients. At each shift change, members of staff would have a 'handover report'. This gave the necessary information to be able to care for the patient, and monitor their illness; four hourly temperature, pulse, and respirations (TPR) and blood pressure (BP), known as Obs (observations). During the first three days, patients were to be on strict bed rest – meaning they could only get up for the commode. After three days, their time up was increased according to their condition. So from the fourth day, it may be for one hour, morning and afternoon.

On this particular day, the gentleman in the first bed had been admitted less than twenty-four hours earlier, which meant that he was on bed rest for another two days. I remember him asking the student nurse for a commode, and she obligingly brought one to him and closed the curtains for his privacy. I turned and carried on with a task that I needed to complete.

A few minutes later, I could hear gasps coming from some of the other men on the ward. As I turned around, I saw them all staring towards the man who had just been given the commode. However, their glances were aimed upwards above the bed, which made me turn and look in the same direction.

To my horror, the learner had taken it literally about the bed rest. Between her and the patient, she had negotiated and positioned the commode on top of the bed, and WORSE, the poor man was pinioned on top of the commode. Because of the combined height of the bed and commode, his terrified face could be seen above the curtains, and just the one hand waving frantically for help (the other hand was firmly gripping the commode). I don't remember much noise coming from his lips; I put this down to his utter terror at the time.

The student nurse had admirably ensured his cardiac monitor leads remained on his chest, even moving the machine a little closer to him, to prevent the electrodes pinging off. The commode, to say the least, was very unsteady, a soft mattress not being conducive to stability.

For a few seconds I was dumb struck but my training served me well. I and a couple of other colleagues sprang into action, appearing calm as we gently slid him from the commode to the relative safety of the mattress, shielding the back of his head from the commode wheels. Two of us supported him, while another two managed to move the commode back to ground level.

By the time we had done all this, his need for the loo had increased. On this occasion, we were given the doctor's approval to wheel him to the toilet at the end of the ward. Although remaining speechless, his face expressed sincere gratitude at being allowed this perk after his recent trauma.

The Pager

As the months went on, I continued to learn and grow in my role as a staff nurse. My NFE was almost perfected – or so I thought.

Many things have changed over the years but the consultant's Ward Round remains almost the same, with only minor changes. There were often four or five different consultants who had patients on the ward. One consultant in particular, a small man but quite stern and very business-like, arrived to see his patients and to review their care and treatment. The retinue consisted of the consultant, his senior registrar, junior registrar, and the house officer. These medics were backed up by the ward sister, staff nurse, and student nurses.

The ward was wholly silent when these rounds went on, apart from the odd patient who was oblivious to the event. Each patient was seen in turn. The consultant would take a verbal report from the registrars, the notes would be read and decisions made for ongoing treatment. The whole process was one of total concentration. All involved would make notes of the instructions issued for the next phase of treatment. The patient would only be allowed to speak when spoken to.

On this particular day, the junior doctor (who was on-call) would invariably carry his pager, known by most staff as his 'bleep'. This was, and still is, a way of contacting the doctor to summon his help or advice. Because the consultant's round was so important, it was frowned upon for the doctor to go to the phone and discover why he was needed, other than in emergencies. To this end, the student nurse, being on the lower echelons of rank, was asked by the ward sister to 'answer the bleep'. The doctor concerned nodded gratefully.

Slowly, the learner made her way round the bed, and towards the doctor with the bleep. Perhaps she was checking his name. Her eyes darted across the white coated doctors and appeared to be frantically searching for the bleep. To her obvious relief, it sounded again and she could identify the owner. Slowly, she inched closer to his chest, which puzzled me intensely. I was about to confirm to her that the bleep which needed answering did indeed belong to that particular junior doctor. She paused and then stood stock still. I nodded to her to reassure her that she had identified the medic whose pager needed answering. At this point, I made space so she could exit to the ward telephone to pick up his messages.

I glanced away only for a second or two, and then heard, in a very loud voice, a shout of, "H E L L O!" aimed at the doctor's top pocket.

The consultant's round had been going quite smoothly until then. The doctor stepped back quickly in surprise, lost his balance and tripped into the registrars. The registrars tried to avoid colliding and promptly stood on my foot.

Despite the disruption, and minor injuries among the retinue, the consultant seemed unconcerned. He uttered nothing in response to the disruption but merely carried on as though a small fly had passed by and needed a waft of air to send it on its way. However, the student nurse was mortified, I have never seen anyone before or after with so much colour in their cheeks. If she is still around today, this incident must be etched in her memory forever.

BACK TO THE VALLEY AND A NEW JOB

Moving Back Home

After twelve months of post-registration experience, I moved to the Rossendale Valley, back to my roots, where my family lived.

I had applied and was successful in gaining a position on Ward 14 at Rossendale General Hospital. In years gone by, the hospital had been a workhouse. It was where the 'paupers' lived and worked. I had read somewhere that it was normal to separate families by gender. They grew their own food, ate simple diets. Breakfast would be porridge and supper would be oat biscuits made from the leftovers. The men worked there, and provided the labour to feed the families. The women washed and cooked with what facilities there were. According to one historian, the men were paid in tobacco – four ounces a week.

When I arrived at the hospital, the tower and clock were still very visible landmarks, easily seen from a distance.

Ethel

There was one other legacy from the workhouse days, and that legacy turned out to be longstanding patients. Ethel was one of these patients and had spent all her life in a wheelchair because of spina bifida, which caused paralysis from her waist down.

My first post at the hospital was as a staff nurse on the geriatric ward, as it was called in those days. Some of the characters remain etched in my memory. I feel there are three in particular whose charisma must be shared with the reader.

My first meeting with Ethel was in the corridor of the ward where I was newly appointed. She smiled sweetly at me, and appeared confident and content. As it turned out, Ethel was top dog on that ward. There was nothing wrong with her thinking or powers of deduction.

I still feel that any new member of staff on the ward was vetted by her. It seemed that Ethel had to be the first in the queue for any attention that was given to the patients. She had been born at the latter end of the workhouse days, and had been 'inherited' when it became a hospital in the 1970s. When I first began working there, she was in her seventies, so I'm guessing she may have been born at the turn of the century, around 1900.

Ethel knew about each patient, each member of staff and anyone of importance who could be used to make her life a little more comfortable. In most cases, the workhouse inmates were resettled into community homes. Ethel unfortunately was not relocated. Eventually she chose to stay in the place that was familiar to her.

The ward was made up of four mini wards; each had about eight beds. There was a mixture of conditions, from strokes to dementia and many other illnesses that were classed as long term. Ethel was as independent as she could be, considering she was paralysed and had deformed lower limbs. However, her upper body made up for this. She wheeled herself up and down the main corridor on the ward like a Roman Centurion.

I had decided (unfortunately) I was not going to allow her to rule the roost when I was on duty and that she would take her turn like everyone else. I sat down to explain that at that time, some conditions which patients suffered from needed more intense care than she did. Therefore, it could be another hour or so before we could tend to her routine needs. She looked at me sweetly and nodded that she understood. I remember thinking to myself that I deserved a pat on the back; I had her understanding of the matter, and we could tend to the patients in order of priority.

A couple of days later I walked down the corridor as Ethel was approaching from the other end in her chair. Believing that we now had an understanding, I nodded and smiled as she moved herself forward. She had just been issued with an electric wheelchair, which allowed her to move with ease. I remember her being quite a rotund lady, filling the chair easily. As we met in the corridor, I stood back to let her wheel past me. I regretted that move deeply. I had my back against the wall, and my feet pointing into the corridor. The initial pain took me by surprise. It seemed to travel up from my toes to about my shin. As I moved the affected foot in the air, more as a reflex action, she quickly manoeuvred her wheelchair and skilfully ran over my other foot.

At this point I must have appeared to be dancing. I glanced at Ethel as she smiled sweetly back at me and apologised profusely for the 'accident'. When the other staff on the ward heard about the incident, there seemed to be little in the way of surprise at Ethel's escapade. There was an awkward silence until one of the staff spluttered out, "We forgot to tell you, if Ethel doesn't like you, she will run over your feet!"

From that point onwards, I was very careful not to cross paths with Ethel.

Peggy

On the same ward, but a very different personality, was Peggy. She had been there for a few years, and was in her eighties when she was admitted. At a guess, she was probably born in the late 1880s. She suffered from dementia, but had a lovely disposition. After living in the area for seventy years, she still had a strong Irish accent.

Peggy was immobile and unable to walk or stand. In fact, she could have been described as 'chair shaped'. She knew enough to understand that she was in a hospital ward, and we were nurses. Her favourite pastime was counting and she would repeatedly count to one hundred and two. For some unknown reason, she always missed the number one hundred out, going from ninety-nine to one hundred and one. I never found out why. Her visitors used to bring in sweets and chocolates. They would place them on her bedside locker in a glass dish so she could reach them as she lay in bed.

Sometimes, as the students washed and dressed the patients, they would be offered sweets by them as a token of gratitude. I usually advised against accepting these sweets unless they were wrapped. Peggy was to prove my point beyond any reasonable doubt. On one particular morning, she appeared to have some rum truffles in a dish on her locker. As the curtains were drawn to give her a bed bath and dress her, she ceremoniously routed under her bedclothes and very neatly added another 'rum truffle' to her collection. On further examination of her dish of sweets, she had added another half dozen 'truffles' to it. However, the truffles were not as they appeared and, pulling the sheets back, Peggy had been invading her anatomy and disposing of her 'truffles' in an endearing fashion; by mixing them with the others on her locker. Hence the instructions "DON'T ACCEPT UNWRAPPED SWEETS."

I tried to make time to get to know these elderly people, who once functioned and worked just as we did. Quite often, the long term memory is better than trying to remember what happened two hours earlier. On one occasion, I sat next to Peggy and asked what it was she did for a living in her younger years. I was saddened and surprised to hear her utter "I used to go whoring in Rawtenstall train station."

She was so matter of fact about it. I guess it must have been around the time of the First World War. I realise that this type of work has existed for hundreds of years, but it still shocked me to hear this ninety-six year-old lady tell me what she had done to earn money.

Still Doing the Job

Because there were four separate bays within the ward, we were able to nurse men as well as women. Many of them suffered from dementia, but came under the umbrella of 'geriatric' patients. It was understandable that relatives struggled to deal with the behaviour of their loved ones.

One day as I pushed the drug trolley into the male ward, I began to give out the tablets as normal. The student nurses helped to administer these tablets to the patients. As I looked up from the drug sheets, I caught one man wandering from bed to bed, looking at each patient intently before moving to the next one. Before I could do anything, he started measuring up the first bedfast occupant. He seemed intent on getting the length and breadth of the sleeping occupant. He appeared to do this with all the men who had fallen asleep, as they often did after their midday meal.

As he completed the measurement of the third and final sleeping body, he turned and went back to his bed. He proceeded to write on a piece of paper the results of his actions. He didn't speak while measuring or report on his completed task. I was curious to say the least, but knew that asking him directly may not have yielded answers. He hadn't harmed or upset anyone (his subjects had remained asleep). As I returned to the office, I started looking through his notes to see if he had done anything similar in the past. It didn't appear that anyone had noted this behaviour in him. I was intrigued, but nothing had been documented.

I noticed many patients with dementia had travelled back in time, to when they were working, and exhibited behaviours related to their work. In some cases it was obvious that they were back in the cotton mills, working and weaving away on invisible looms, or a miner working the caves and collecting coal.

I looked at the information in the measurer's notes and suddenly it all made sense. It was a little unnerving to discover that his lifelong job had been that of an undertaker! He'd been measuring up the bodies in order to find a suitable coffin! I was so glad that the 'bodies' didn't awaken during the exercise. It was bad enough being in a hospital, without waking up to someone measuring you for your casket.

The Shepherd

In the same ward, another man aged around seventy-five was also very busy, but in a very different way. Another nurse and I were making the beds one morning, when we heard a thud on the floor. As we looked up from the bed making, we could see a woman prostrate on the floor, rubbing her knees. It was the ward cleaner. We dashed over to check her over for injuries and to help her up. She was looking at the seventy-five year old man who was grinning seated in his chair. The cleaner explained how she came to fall, and it was no accident. The man had turned his stick around, so that the crook end was on the floor. He was still in attack mode and looking for another victim. It seemed he thought that everyone was out to get him and he sat there in wait to inflict more damage on passers-by. He had decided that if he couldn't walk or stand, he would hook his stick around the victim's ankle and give it an almighty yank.

I felt that this man needed a few words to explain to him that what he was doing wasn't very nice and was also dangerous and unkind. I knelt down in front of him so as to not intimidate him. I gently asked him to stop tripping people up. I regretted this move immediately. His hands at this point were resting on his knee. My neck was therefore comparatively close to his hands. As I started to speak, he moved his hands upwards and then around my neck. For his age, he had quite a strong grip; it would have been impressive had those hands not been squeezing the air out of my throat.

I managed to extricate myself, and decided the next call would be to the doctor on duty. Luckily for the ward, and me, the man was transferred to the psychiatric unit within a couple of hours!

NIGHT DUTY

Creative skills

After gaining some more experience of care and management on that very special ward, I decided to apply for another position, to be a night staff nurse, on the female acute medical ward.

To get to know how things were done and what the routines were, I learned the ropes by first working on the day shifts for a month or so.

Nursing at night is very different and though the hospital didn't have an Accident and Emergency Department, we took transfers from the local A&E along with GP urgent admissions. It could be very busy at times, to say the least. The routines were much the same on most of the wards, and our medical teams were available twenty-four hours a day, seven days a week. The junior doctors worked some very long hours, sometimes with little or no sleep (the laws and recommendations regarding the number of hours they could be on call changed later). So usually, after doing ward rounds all day, dealing with GP admissions, and trying to sort out ongoing problems, those doctors became exhausted.

I remember one occasion when a poor junior doctor had

been on call all weekend, following his normal, very long working week. It was not unusual at all to see them active for eighty or more hours between Friday evening and Monday morning. Very often they would be called out to the wards for various problems, and not just to one ward; it could be many different wards, according to where the beds were available.

The doctor was hardly able to stand on his feet, and our hearts went out to him. We would make him hot drinks and sandwiches to keep him going. On many occasions, as soon as he had returned to his room in the doctors' quarters within the hospital grounds, he would be called out again.

As I saw him stagger onto the ward, I made my mind up to try to help him the best I could. We had one empty side ward (it was actually a single bedded room on the main ward). When the doctor had done what he had to do, I beckoned him to the room and told him to rest as much as he could. The poor man was too tired to eat or drink, and within three or four minutes he was fast asleep. He managed about three hours sleep before his next call, but at least he was already on the ward. I guess he may well be at the latter end of his career as a consultant now. I am sure he will recall his time as a junior doctor with mixed memories.

Melaena Stool

It was common for doctors to catch up with writing patients' notes and reviewing prescriptions during the late evening and at night. One doctor was not particularly friendly and, when offered a drink and food, would not speak. He ignored us and generally treated the nurses as necessary but inferior.

After a month or two, I decided I would create a situation which would grab his immediate attention. I arranged with the nursing auxiliary to 'create a medical problem', which would need his attention. Firstly it is necessary to describe a condition called melaena stool.

This is a condition of the gastro-intestinal tract, and indicates that the patient has bled internally. Because the bleed happens higher up the bowel, there is no evidence of blood. A tarry black semi-liquid stool is passed. In any event, it is a serious condition, and warrants immediate attention and investigations.

INGREDIENTS FOR MELAENA STOOL

1. Receptacle - Cardboard bedpan liner.
2. Ingredients - Jardox (beef tea), similar in consistency and looks to Marmite.
3. Toilet paper - with a dabbing of Jardox on it.
4. Fictitious name - written on bedpan.
5. Final ingredient - a couple of fruit gums gently buried in the Jardox.

I prepared the bedpan and invented a coded signal, which would indicate to the auxiliary nurse to bring the specimen to my attention.

The stage was set and the doctor appeared at his usual time. He walked straight past us, and started to work his way through the patients' notes. I asked him if he would like a drink or a biscuit. As usual, he ignored the offer.

The pre-arranged sign was given to summon the auxiliary nurse (Sheila), to the office with the bedpan. She then informed me that Mrs Bloggs had just passed the specimen. Looking appropriately concerned, Sheila asked me if it could be melaena stool. I felt the doctor's eyes move and focus on the bedpan. I took it in my hands and inhaled deeply, responding that it did indeed smell like melaena stool (more reaction from the doctor).

I put my hand inside the bedpan, and took out a small lump, very slowly putting it in my mouth and letting it move around to get the full flavour (and effect). I then told Sheila how grateful I was, that she had brought this to my attention, as it certainly tasted like melaena stool.

Until this point, the doctor had remained riveted to his chair. I turned to offer him the bedpan, at which point he was on his feet and had taken a couple of steps back. His chair seemed to find its way to the back wall and rolled haphazardly into the desk. As I looked towards the doctor, despite the lights being dimmed, his face changed colour. He produced a triad of shades in white, red and green. The most dominant one, I felt, was green.

He seemed to shuffle sideways past me; I assumed it was an attempt to avoid the bedpan. I observed that his interest in it had diminished, and was superseded by his need to leave the ward. My last sighting of him was seeing his white coat flapping down the corridor, muttering something about the nurse eating s**t.

I was told that he meticulously checked my duty rota to avoid having any further encounters with me. *I never saw him again.*

The Obese Admission

Some months later, one of the junior doctors (a very nice man) decided to play a trick on me. My little prank had become known throughout the hospital and most knew that I enjoyed the lighter side of nursing.

The shift began in its usual manner, by settling all the patients down ready for the night. It was one of the nights where we were on call to take emergency admissions. The doctor had been to the ward to update some notes, and we had the usual friendly banter with him. Around 3 a.m. as most of the patients were sleeping, the doctor rang the ward, asking us to prepare a bed for an urgent admission.

We were told that the patient was very large, and would not fit in a normal sized hospital bed. He requested that we put two beds together, and then place the mattresses laterally, which could then be held in place by bed sheets. After about fifteen minutes, we had prepared the bed(s) to accommodate our obese patient. Everything had been prepared, even to the point of providing the biggest night dress you could imagine (otherwise known as a theatre gown).

We then awaited the ambulance which would deliver our patient to the specially made-up bed. Time went by, and we continued with the routine care for the other patients. Around 6 a.m. the doctor arrived on the ward, and decided to check out all the preparations we had made for the admission. He smiled and commented on the excellent job we had done. About an hour later (or should I say an hour before the day shift arrived?) our pleasant doctor announced that the patient had been transferred to a different hospital, and the bed(s) were no longer needed. We quickly returned them to their original state, before the shift change over.

He never did let on that the whole thing was a prank. He had confided in the ward sister what he had done, but continued his silence until he left after his three month secondment. Only then were we informed that the joke was on us! He had been told of my melaena stool episode, and didn't want me to reciprocate his trick, with one of my own. I certainly had a giggle about it, and after all, 'If you can't take it, don't give it!'

A Slight Language Barrier

I chose to train and become a nurse when major changes were taking place in the health service. Out went the matron; in came the nursing officer. Equipment changed. Much of our time was spent in cleaning re-useable items, from washing and drying bandages to disinfecting the metal bedpans and glass urinals. As a student nurse it was a relief to be out of sight of the ward sister while we did our chores in the sluice. Some of this archaic equipment was still in use after I qualified and at night it was difficult to clean up, as the noise from the sluice kept patients awake. The bedpans and urinals would be put in the sluice room and, when enough had been collected, cleansed and sterilised ready for re-use. However, if someone had a bowel movement, we did immediately clean the bedpan or commode.

One night we were doing our settling down round, issuing clean glass urinals to the men, and frequently placing a commode next to a patient's bed. This ensured that they could pee and poo whenever they desired. As we collected the used pans and urinals, it became glaringly obvious that a Polish gentleman hadn't got the gist of what the urinal was for. We were intrigued and surprised when we surveyed the glass urinal, with its contents. My colleague and I looked on in amazement. How had he managed to do that?! He must've been in a strange position, did he stand? Did he sit? If so, where?

Our questions were endless. In our minds we envisaged the dynamics of 'how did he manage that?' The patient was ambulant, but we needed him to pee in a urinal, so we could measure the amount of fluid he passed. As we took the bottle to the sluice, the question 'HOW?' came to mind. But not just how he managed to get it in the urinal, but more importantly, how did we get it out? There, in all its glory, was the largest stool you could imagine, neatly curled round and round inside the bottle. It took quite some time to remove the offending item, and return the urinal to its former state. And finally, our Polish man had to be approached and shown which bit of his anatomy was meant to fill the bottle.

He's Coming Home with Us

As in all nurses' experiences, death and dying is an unavoidable part of our work when the end of life approaches. Many times, we tend the dying, hoping to give peace and dignity as they travel to their final destination. The needs of the relatives and patients are so important. A person's memories of how their loved one departed will remain with them. When a patient is no longer able to sustain life, it is our task to ensure that comfort and dignity is maintained. One such occasion from way back in the early days of my nursing career remains in my memory.

As I arrived for the night shift, it was quite obvious that someone had passed from this world. We took the report at the shift handover and it was confirmed that Mr Smith in the first bed had died. The bed curtains were closed and the relatives were waiting in a small room on the corridor.

It was my job to confirm the name of the undertakers and arrange for the body to be taken to the mortuary where it would be collected by the funeral staff. This was usually arranged with the relatives, while they were given refreshments and time to adjust. It was about midnight when the most senior member of the family approached me and requested – no, insisted – that they were taking the deceased home in their car. Until this point in my career, I had never come across a situation that sent me into 'Oh my God!' mode. However, this was definitely a situation which rendered me almost speechless.

As in previous times, my NFE appeared, but this time it was to mask my shock and surprise at the request made by the family. I gave them another pot of tea, mainly to keep them occupied. I regrouped and went on to contact my nursing officer, the doctor and anyone else deemed appropriate who could discuss this request.

On this occasion, it was declared that the death was by natural causes. Eventually, permission was given for the family to remove the body and take it home.

The usual procedure on a Florence Nightingale ward was to close all the patients' bed curtains whilst the body was taken to the mortuary by the hospital porters. On this occasion, it was the relatives who took the lead. Their car was parked outside the fire doors at the rear end of the ward, a wheelchair was placed next to the bed and the male members of the family proceeded to dress Mr Smith in jacket and trousers. This was not an easy task as rigor mortis was beginning to set in and the once flaccid body was becoming less than manoeuvrable.

Eventually, the deceased was placed in the wheelchair, complete with flat cap. I cannot begin to imagine how difficult it was to get him on the back seat of the car, but we couldn't leave the ward unattended to help with this.

After the family left, I began to wonder about all the things that could have gone wrong, especially on their way back home. If something did go wrong, we didn't hear about it. The thought of pulling up at traffic lights and the driver of another car peering innocently into theirs doesn't bear thinking about. I did wonder what the police would've done or said, had they pulled over the vehicle.

Much later on, I discovered that it is traditional for the Irish to take their loved ones home, and begin the wake around the open coffin. The police should have been informed. However, at that time I was a little less experienced in these matters and found it all quite unnerving. To this day, my imagination runs riot at the thought of the family taking Mr Smith home and how they managed to get him out of the car at the other end.

ON THE DISTRICT

My New World of Nursing.

After spending a couple years gaining more experience as a staff nurse, I felt it was a time to change my direction and to specialise in district nursing. This was to mean a further twelve months college training, at the end of which I would be a district nursing sister. I would have a case load of my own and be attached to a GP surgery. By now, it was 1989 and I was excited to be chosen to attend the course which, if I was successful, would be followed by three months supervised practice.

After qualifying, I was allocated to a small GP practice in Burnley where I was the only district nurse, so had to organise the workload and actually do it all too. I was later moved to a larger health centre, where I worked alongside a full team of district nurses.

We were employed by the Health Authority and not by GPs, so had a similar echelon of managers overseeing the district nurse teams as in a hospital setting. However, the GPs were able to give us direct referrals of patients, whom we would visit and assess in the community.

District nursing is very different from anything in a

hospital. The first thing to remember is that you are entering into someone's home, effectively as a guest; you must have permission to enter their living quarters. It is also worth mentioning that in this area of nursing we visited the whole spectrum of patients, from the very rich to the very poor and all those in between.

Mobile phones were new and had not been introduced into the health service as a useful tool and therefore, there was little or no communication with the team. It was only when we met up after the morning visits that we could share and update the information we had about our patients.

It was also part of our role to run the treatment room clinics, where the more ambulant patients could attend to have their care delivered at the surgery. It varied from removal of sutures, to ear syringing, to anything else that our training covered.

The visits to patients were worked out as best we could by geography, frequency and urgency. I enjoyed the variety and nature of the work and, being in the Pennines, the travel into the countryside and the diversity of our patients. Satellite Navigation wasn't part of our equipment and we located our patients by using maps and verbal directions from colleagues. It wasn't unusual for me to get lost and have to knock on doors to ask for directions.

The Wrong Address

One grey morning, I set off to attend and assess a lady who had been discharged from hospital. She needed stitches removing following surgery as an inpatient. One of the most annoying things to contend with was the lack of door numbers on rows of houses. Some had names on (not helpful) and some had nothing. It was a case of having to find just one house with a number on it (preferably two so we could work out which way the numbers ran) thus enabling us to find our patient. I sympathised with the emergency services who urgently had to find addresses. Thank goodness that now, there is the ability to track phone signals to a location.

On this particular day I was aware that many buildings were without numbers, so I laboriously attempted to work out which house I would be visiting. Unfortunately, there were gaps between the rows, and unbeknown to me, some of the houses had been demolished. The area had a few varying shops interspersed between private houses. I finally reached a door which I thought must have belonged to the lady I was to assess. I knocked loudly, but there was no response. I knocked again; still no response. This was a common occurrence as quite often patients would be in a rear room, or were deaf.

I knocked again, and shouted, "It's only the nurse!"

The door was unlocked, so I made my way into a rather dull room. As my eyes adjusted to the light, I realised it was some sort of shop, but not one I was used to. A man standing at the counter peered at me as I walked towards him. There seemed to be a slight smirk on his face as I moved forward. I was acutely aware that I was dressed in my nurse's uniform, complete with the famous black stockings. (Actually, they were thick woolly tights.)

As I glanced around, there was various equipment on show: magazines, films, whips, handcuffs etc. Before I could ask for the lady in question, he beat me to it and pointed to the nurse's uniforms for sale. He probably thought mine was a little dull and mundane compared to the items on his shelves!

Once again I used my NFE, which had become invaluable. In my best nurse's voice, I asked if he knew the address I was after, or if the lady in question lived there. By this time I had caught the attention of a couple of customers, who looked my way with a twinkling in their eyes.

I retreated rapidly to my car, ensuring that I hadn't been followed. I am pleased to say I did eventually find my patient, who was highly amused by my wanderings.

The Bath Assessment

It was quite reassuring that getting a wrong address was not just in the remit of the newly qualified district nursing sister, like me! Our usual meet up at the GP surgery had more than one purpose in those days. Partly, it was good to share the trials and tribulations of our work, along with the pleasant or funny moments.

My more experienced colleague came into the office a few minutes later than was normal, looking a little flustered. She had gone to see a newly referred patient with a view to assessing how the client would manage to have a bath at home. This was a frequent request from the hospital when sending patients home. Ideally we would check if they could get in and out of the bath, if they needed any aids or adaptations or if a district auxiliary nurse needed to go regularly to assist the patient. As frequently happens, some of the referrals did not require any help at all, so the assessment was done first, and then, if needed, all the paperwork was completed.

As my colleague recounted the visit, it appeared to her that the lady would probably be able to manage without any input from the district nurses. The stairs to the bathroom didn't seem to be a hindrance, the lady ran the bath and managed to get both in and out unaided. She appeared more than capable of dressing herself.

It seemed to my colleague that there was no further input needed. As they went to the door my colleague said, "Well, Mrs Jones, I don't think you need any help from us, as you seem to have managed to bathe and dress yourself with ease."

The lady replied in a rather puzzled voice, "But I am Mrs Smith... Mrs Jones lives next door!"

Both parties were at fault, of course, the nurse for not checking the name on arrival and Mrs Smith for just allowing someone to bathe her.

Although a little red faced, my colleague undoubtedly saw the funny side, as did we all.

The Cow

One of the attractions of working on the district was meeting such a wide variety of people. Here is a good example.

On the outskirts of Burnley, farms and houses were dotted around. As in hospitals, student nurses were seconded to various specialties and many chose to experience the work of the district nurse.

I remember quite vividly when a student nurse came with me to visit a sick gentleman who lived on a farm some distance from the road. We had to open a big metal gate to enter the field and dirt track which took us to his farmhouse. I thought it was handy to have the student with me, so she could open the gate. I could drive through, then she could secure it.

The idea was pretty good in theory but I hadn't considered

that the student was terrified of cows. There were probably around a dozen in the field and one in particular seemed interested in what we were doing. However, it was some distance away and didn't appear to be a threat.

By now the student was almost hysterical and so I was left to open the gate, drive through and then close it.

Simple?

I thought so at the time.

I got out of the car and pushed open the gate, returning to the car to move it forward. Just at that instant, the curious cow walked pass us and escaped out onto the road. For a split second I saw all sorts of scenarios, the least of which was a dead cow. Though I knew that nurses carry indemnity insurance, I wasn't sure if it covered escaped, damaged or dead cattle.

I turned on my heel, yelling at the student to close the gate and, at this point, I believe she feared me more than she did the cow.

As I raced down the country lane, dressed in full District Nurses' gear, I was hoping against hope that the cow would see sense and return to the field. But cows don't look at things in quite that way, so I found myself chasing it down the road.

It must have been a strange sight and, luckily, a driver seemed to think there was something odd going on. He slowed down as I legged it after the cow. He mouthed to me, "Are you chasing the cow?"

I felt like saying, "What the hell do you think I'm doing? Going for a jog? In my best uniform?"

Seeing my predicament, he drove down the lane and came to a halt near the cow, which had also stopped. With a few manoeuvres, he managed to turn the escapee back towards the gate. It then seemed to take root on top of a large mound of grass.

As the cow was almost back in the field, the driver went on his way. My car was as I had left it, and the student was back in it (after she had been brave enough to close the gate). Now all I had to do was to open the gate a little and the cow would go through it. At least, that's what I hoped.

I looked at the cow, which towered above me on the mound of grass. Its eyes were wide and staring. I pushed the gate open and, as I glanced at the cow again, it began to pee a very big pee. At this point I knew the cow was more afraid of me, than I was of it. I slapped it on the rear and it moved rapidly into the field. The student just sat there with a stunned look on her face. I guessed she wouldn't be choosing district nursing as a career.

We went into the farmhouse and tended to the patient's needs. Since the cow belonged to a different farmer, the family we were visiting were unaware of the situation, but I still wanted to apologise to the owner. Then during our visit, the phone rang. I watched as the patient picked up the phone. He nodded avidly as he listened to the voice at the other end. It turned out to be the owner of the cow. My patient rented the field to the man on the phone.

After replacing the receiver, he turned towards the student and me. "That worr t'farmer who azz t'cow that tha worr chasin'. 'ee sez to tell yer that ee'z moved t'cows ont' another field, and yer can geet back ont' road bout loozin' any more on em! (That was the farmer who owns the cow you were chasing. He says to let you know that he's moved the cows into another field, and you can now get back to the road without losing any more of them!)

The relief must've been visible on our faces. And so we left, both of us wearing a smile, and beat a hasty retreat. The cow, I believe, was none the worse for its adventure.

Asda Price(less)

It was not unusual to bump into ex-patients when we were not on duty. Like most people, I went shopping on my days off, often to the supermarket. Patients tended to recognise me before I recognised them. We saw scores of patients and remembered many of them, but it was not always the case if our visits were short term.

I remember pushing my trolley around the store, and could feel someone behind me. He then caught up with me, and said, "Nurse, just look at this! It's so much better!"

Even without my uniform on, I had obviously impressed him in the past. I am afraid I just didn't recognise him.

As we stood in the aisle, I smiled at him and said I was very pleased for him; but that was not enough. Right in front of me, he began rolling down his trousers. I was glued to the spot and had great concern about what he was about to show me.

I furtively looked around to see if anyone was watching as he proudly showed me his leg. At some point in the past, I had dressed his wound in the treatment rooms at the surgery. That leg was now bared in Asda supermarket for me to inspect. His trousers, at this point, were around his ankles. I glanced at his leg (which was now healed) and muttered something about being really pleased for him.

I told him I was late for a meeting with a friend, and that I had to go. As I pushed my shopping trolley down the aisle, he slowly started to pull up his trousers. Luckily there were only two or three people in the vicinity.

I rapidly made my way to the checkout and vowed not to use that particular store again.

Animal Magic

Unlike hospitals, the homes we visited often had pets. My next little episode was memorable only because of the odds of it happening were astronomical. However, happen it did, enabling me to write about this lovely entrepreneur.

I was on my daily visits around Burnley and went to see a lady who needed regular injections. Over time, we had gotten to know each other, and would chat as I prepared and gave her injection. On one occasion, she told me of a stray cat which had been visiting her. Feeling sorry for it, she allowed it to bed down in the shed and fed it regularly. It had seemed pleased to be able to rest where there was comparative warmth, shelter and food.

Being a cat lover, I took an interest in Bella, who at first was a little scruffy and unkempt but, after being taken care of, she became friendly and enjoyed being stroked and played with. My visits were worked in order of priority, but often went to patients in the same geographical areas when possible. I had another couple of visits only streets away.

After a few months, the lady who had given Bella refuge became visibly upset. Bella had disappeared one cold November morning. She pleaded with me to keep my eye out for the cat, which she missed enormously.

I went to my next patient, only a few streets away, to give her the three monthly injection her doctor had prescribed. On my arrival, she ushered me into the kitchen where she spent most of her daytime hours. After washing my hands and preparing the injection, I noticed a new lodger in a cat bed by the fire. As I glanced at the occupant, it looked vaguely familiar. Then it dawned on me that here was Bella, who had absconded from her previous home. She had landed in a warmer environment and was free to come and go in the kitchen area. The new owner began to tell me how Bella had meandered through the open door and had made herself comfortable. This new home was much warmer, and more conducive to keeping a cat happy.

I knew winter was on its way and didn't have the heart to say where Bella had been previously. She looked well-fed and comfortable in that little kitchen.

A few months later I visited the two ladies again and I wondered about Bella. As I made my way to the second house, I began to think about the cat, glad that she was in a warm and comfortable home.

As I went in the kitchen to prepare the injection, I noticed that the bed had gone, so of course I enquired after Bella (who had by then, been given a new name). The lady became a little upset, saying that one day Bella had left the kitchen and didn't return as normal. She asked that I keep an out for her, concerned that she could have been hit by a car or just lost.

I began thinking about the poor cat, which had just found a warm home and regular food. She then lost them all when she went wandering outside. I found myself looking for dead furry bodies as I made my way a further few streets away to a gentleman who was also needed injections. As I entered his house he welcomed me and sat me down in the front room, eager to tell me about what had recently happened to him. As I listened, I saw movement coming from the sofa, a tail flicking and a very familiar cat stretched out and purring loudly.

It seemed that Bella had wandered into the man's house and pulled very hard on his heart strings. She had found yet another home. Knowing cats quite well, I concluded that Bella had found her forever home with the gentleman. The reasons I felt, were as follows:

1. The first house she lived at would only allow Bella in the outside shed and despite it being safe, it probably was not quite warm enough.

2. The second house allowed Bella into the kitchen. This was a better option, was warm, had plenty of food and the odd stroke and pamper. However she had to stay in the kitchen.

3. The third house was warm, Bella had lots of food, lots of strokes and nursing and free reign in any part of the house. In fact, Bella slept with her new owner and appeared VERY settled.

I was aware that the previous two owners missed Bella very much, but I could understand her moving on and she did indeed find her 'forever home' with the gentleman, who adored her. Being a cat owner myself, I knew too well that this little pussy cat was finally happy and content and would not be moving again. Her new name was Cinders, because she was going to turn into his Cinderella.

Just so the two ladies would stop worrying about Bella, I told a white lie: that I'd heard through the grapevine that the original owners had been searching for her, and she was now safe in her own home.

I cannot begin to work out the odds of me being witness to the amblings of that lovely feline, but I was. I am also sure that she spent the rest of her days being loved and spoiled which, of course, is every cat's dream.

My Car is Dirty

It was part of the job to deal with people from all walks of life – from high up business people to the poverty-stricken, many of whom lived on council house estates. Some of the neighbours could be difficult to deal with; they led hard lives and knew how to protect themselves. Dealing with some of them was just not possible. It was not considered healthy to cross them. Even the cats went around in twos!

One particular day I was visiting one of my regulars, who needed a dressing replaced to a leg ulcer. I had become accustomed to making furtive glances out of the window to check my car was where I had left it and in good condition.

I noticed two or three children climbing all over it. They were around eight years old, and had absconded from school. They seemed to be having great fun as they climbed on the bonnet and roof, and then slid down onto the ground – a game they repeated.

Now this was a tricky one. I didn't want to go storming out telling them to get off and play somewhere else. To do this could possibly lead them to becoming more heavy handed and vandalising my car. In a moment of inspiration, I calmly went out and approached them. They gave me a look of total insolence. I braced myself and with my NFE firmly fixed in place, I called to them. "What will your mum say about you getting your clothes all mucky? My car needs a good wash, and you're getting your clothes pretty dirty."

Their faces changed as if to say, 'This woman has saved us from being grounded and possibly worse...'

Within twenty seconds, they became grateful for being saved from the wrath of mum AND I became their heroine.

They slid off my car and stood up, checking for dirt on their clothing. I confirmed that they had managed to keep reasonably clean. The scowls became grins, and they were all spluttering and saying, "Thanks, Missus."

Nowhere in my district nurse training did they tell me about being creative and diplomatic to get around sticky situations!

The Best Pain Relieving Gel Ever

As a district nurse, I worked alternate weekends. Besides the usual administration of eye drops (up to three times a day), there were other patients who needed care seven-days-a-week. Those who were terminally ill needed the support of all available staff. Besides the regular visits at weekends, we would get requests from the on call doctor, who felt that the district nurse could check out a problem before he had to visit.

One such call came one Sunday morning. The GP doing the on call was quite busy. He asked if I could go and check out a patient who had complained of a sore shoulder. The couple were in their mid-eighties and the lady, it seemed, was in pain due to arthritis in her shoulder.

After the initial weekend visits to my regular patients, I made my way to the address given by the GP. I approached the little back street in Burnley, and found space to park. Retrieving my nurse's bag of tricks, I made my way to the house. The slightly-built husband was waiting at the door for me and he ushered me in to the hallway. Just as we were about to go into the lounge where his wife was, he proudly announced, "I've rubbed it with TAMPAX, and it seems a lot better."

I stopped in my tracks and, wearing my much needed nurse's facial expression, I repeated the statement he had just made. "So you've rubbed it with Tampax?"

All sorts of visions passed through my mind, but my face did not change (very proud moment)! We walked into the lounge together and his wife greeted me, telling me her shoulder was much better after using the Tampax.

I glanced around – looking for the item in question, and asked the husband to show me what he'd used to alleviate the pain.

"Certainly nurse," he said.

Going into the kitchen to retrieve the remedy. I waited in anticipation of what I would be shown.

He returned holding a tube of cream and gave it to me. As I read the label, it dawned on me what had happened. I grinned from ear to ear, and told him that I thought this particular cream was excellent at giving pain relief. It clearly stated on the tube, TRAXAM – Apply up to four times a day.

The lady seemed happy that the 'Tampax' was working and apologised for calling the GP surgery at weekend. I hadn't the heart to say anything about the mispronunciation. And of course, there was the added bonus someone else would derive a smile from the re-naming of the anti-arthritis cream.

Together Forever

I believe that the most enjoyable part of district nursing was the unpredictability of it all. On one particular visit, when the days were getting shorter and the clouds were thick in the skies, I accepted with pleasure the offer of a cuppa from my patient.

He lived alone and seemed as if he needed some conversation and a friendly face. I too was ready for a sit down and a hot drink. We chatted about this and that and he told me about his wife who had passed away a few years earlier. Eventually he told me that he had decided to get a furry companion to keep him company. He acquired a feline friend named Mitzie. She sounded as though she had loads of personality and plenty of loving ways. I understood fully what he meant.

"She's upstairs, shall I bring her down?"

I was more than happy to meet Mitzie, who sounded to be quite a character to say the least. I could hear him moving about in the bedroom, but cats are notorious for playing hide and seek, so I waited patiently to meet Mitzie.

Eventually I could hear footsteps as he came down the stairs. As he re-entered the living room, I felt something was not quite as it should be. My patient was holding a small brown suitcase, which he placed in front of me on the coffee table. It was either a very strange pet carrier, or something else?

As he opened the case, he sort of half-smiled. "I'm going to have her buried with me."

As I took a closer look there was no movement. Then, in a split second, it dawned on me what he meant. Mitzie, it seemed, had died two years earlier. As he lifted up the body I could clearly see that this cat had been well and truly stuffed. The taxidermist had been very busy but not as painstaking as he could have been.

As Mitzie was placed on the table, the full glory of the taxidermist's work came to light. If Mitzie had retained the ability to see, she would've been able to look to the left and to the right at the same time, but not straight ahead. Her tail, which once would have stood high, or swished this way and that, was now virtually folded in two and her fur seemed to be growing the wrong way.

Once again, I had to wear my NFE, and proceeded to lie about how lovely she looked. The owner was oblivious to the failings of Mitzie's makeover, and all I could do was utter a few guttural noises indicating my approval. I did, in the end, manage to tell the man how touching it was, to have his cat with him in the coffin when it was his turn to depart this life.

Even now, after twenty years, I have a very clear vision of Mitzie staring at opposite sides of the room at the same time. I hope that the taxidermist managed to perfect his techniques before the next pet was sentenced to being a contortionist forever.

Fiery Jack.

With most of us, there are occasions when we take alternative medicines to avoid having to go to the doctor. Quite often these remedies have a calming effect on us, just knowing we are doing something for ourselves. However, there is always an exception to the rule.

I was asked to visit a man who had been to the A&E department. His address was on the outskirts of Burnley and I managed to find it easily. The referral came through to me as a wound check. This meant that I was to examine the affected area and decide if ongoing treatment by the nurse was relevant.

I knocked on the door and it was answered by the man's wife. She was a very pleasant lady who seemed a little concerned by her husband's 'problem'. She informed me that they had been married more than forty years and never had to deal with anything similar. She was obviously quite embarrassed as she started to tell me the history behind her husband's affliction. John, as I will call him, sat silently whilst his wife went on to explain the circumstances which brought about the need for my visit.

I made myself comfortable and gave her my full attention while occasionally glancing at John, who seemed to not want to discuss the matter. It soon became clear why this was so. John had been suffering from a bad back for some years. After doing some gardening, he began to feel more pain at the base of his spine. Not one to be calling the doctor, he decided he would try a newly acquired home remedy called Fiery Jack. This cream is no longer available and was discontinued around 2012. Its very name indicated its effect and, when applied, it reached deep into the muscles, giving the heat that was indicated on the tin. John had been quite pleased with the effects and used it a second time to reinforce its power.

By this time, the man was looking down towards his feet and we had no eye contact, so I knew something untoward was about to be said. I turned back to look at his wife and she went on to tell me that the second application seemed to do the trick (at this point she had a little grin on her face). Her husband, it transpired, needed to use the toilet after putting on the second application and so went upstairs to have a pee. Then it happened.

His wife continued, saying that she could hear her husband groaning. He told her to get upstairs quickly. Arriving at the bathroom, she could see that he had wrapped his 'wedding tackle' in a big wet towel. At first she couldn't make out what had happened. Then it dawned on her; he'd gone straight to the loo after applying the Fiery Jack, and hadn't washed his hands.

The result was that his privates were now 'on fire'! John was hopping about in pain and there was no reasoning with him. He yelled that he wanted an ambulance to take him to hospital. His wife decided it was his own fault and said that he would get a taxi there, and not waste the taxpayer's money.

So John had to agree, and the wife gave him first aid. This came as a bowl of cold water, which he had to lay his 'wedding tackle' in, to alleviate the burning sensation.

The taxi firms were used to strange calls, and many requests were made to get people to the local A&E Department. On this occasion, his wife thought the taxi driver was very intrigued by John's delicate condition. The cold water was obviously doing what it was meant to do and so John decided to travel in the back of a taxi, with his 'bits' in the cold water. His wife threw a towel over the offending area and left him to go on his own.

Luckily for me, my NFE had started to kick in automatically as I listened to the story. John was looking a little sheepish by now.

I turned to him, asking the usual questions about his 'wound'. There really wasn't much I could do at this point.

The hospital had given him antiseptic cream and general advice. So, with lounge curtains closed for privacy, John lay on the settee and pulled his very loose trousers down.

It wasn't a pretty sight and I perfectly understood why he travelled with his 'wedding tackle' in a bowl of water. I decided to let his wife take over and apply the cream; we would call back in another week to see if the problem was resolving. Any changes for the worse, they could call up the surgery and we would come straight away.

As I left the house, John's wife followed me to see me to the door. She had a very wry smile on her face. As I went outside, she whispered in my ear, "He washes his hands all the time now – fancy that!"

A Pain in the Rear

When you visit people in their homes, you have to take the rough and the smooth together. Being an animal lover, it was great meeting different pets. I came across many various shapes, sizes and types of animals, from snakes to parrots and all the 'normal' ones in between. Mostly they were friendly and just curious. At the time I did my district nursing, the law had changed and owners could no longer put a 'Beware of the Dog' sign up. To do so meant, in law, that you knowingly had a dangerous animal. Many used to put a little notice on their doors saying: 'My dog can make it to the bottom of the garden in five seconds, can you?' At least this way, we knew we were entering a house with animals.

One such house had five dogs which seemed pretty friendly. Normally patients would put their animals in another room until the nurse had done what she came to do. However, on this occasion the dogs were free to roam around the property. I carried on with the leg dressing uninterrupted; on completion, the owner stayed in her living room. I made my way to the front door at the end of the corridor. That's where my freedom to move ended. The dogs surrounded me as I went to open the door. The woman was still in the living room but couldn't hear me shouting to her. As I looked down, the five dogs were staring at me. Every time I went to open the door they growled deep, throaty growls that were hardly audible. I could see I wasn't going to get out of there easily, nor could I go back towards the woman. I had my nurse's bag with me, so I put it between me and the nearest dog, which looked like he/she was ready to pounce. As I tried to keep that dog at bay I felt a burning sharp pain in my right buttock. This time it was me that let out a yelp, not the dog. I felt an oozing of something warm and wet running down my thigh, then down my leg. I swung around to the dog that had bitten me and, keeping my grip on my bag, brought it down heavily on the offender's head.

Near the front door there was another door leading off. I tried the handle, hoping this was somewhere I could shelter from the pack of dogs. Luck was on my side because the handle turned and I found sanctuary. I shut the door hastily to prevent being followed by the dogs. The one which had been hit with my bag wasn't happy (but then, neither was I). Once I recovered from the shock, I realised that I could feel a deep and painful throbbing in my rear end and the trickle of blood had made its way further down my leg.

Eventually, I composed myself and proceeded to shout loudly to the lady I had just left in the other room. Because of the stranger in their midst, the dogs now started to bark loudly, and the woman eventually appeared in front of me. After putting the pack securely in another room, she opened the door to where I had found safety. I'm not sure if she was more concerned about her dogs, or about me. She proceeded to say that they were good dogs really, and must have been scared. I remember thinking that they were not alone on that score. Finally I made my way out and decided to go back to the surgery, where I had to ask one of the GPs to check over my bite injury. This was quite embarrassing as I worked with him and wasn't actually his patient. However, he was very discreet and suggested I check that my tetanus injections were up to date.

After reporting the incident to my nursing officer, it turned out that the dogs had attacked other people, and the police had been involved. I never went back again and neither did any of my colleagues. The woman was informed that if she wanted treating, someone would have to take her to the surgery. My pride and dignity did eventually heal.

Mrs Miggins

In warm, balmy summer days, I loved travelling to the outreaches of Pendle. There were some stunning country villages and the fields were ablaze with buttercups and daisies. Even Pendle Hill, despite the infamous witches, was picturesque. On a day filled with warm sunshine, I went to visit a young man in his early thirties who had been diagnosed with testicular cancer. He'd already had the necessary surgery and I was there purely to check his wound and assess if he needed any other support from us. The operation meant he was now sterile, but some sperm had been saved and frozen in the hope that one day he would father a child.

I placed my bag on the floor and sat down; the bag was open as I was anticipating needing some bits out of it to re-dress his wound. It was a leisurely visit, and we had a long chat about what the diagnosis and surgery had meant to him.

Because having a child was not certain, he had decided to get a gorgeous little kitten which he called Mrs Miggins. At that time she was just a playful fluff ball, but I could see he loved her very much. I took out the dressings from my bag, and we went into the bedroom. All was fine with my lovely young patient and I packed up my stuff and fastened my bag ready to go. We had spent a pleasant half hour, not rushing as was usual, and I bade him goodbye.

As I set off, I did my usual check to ensure that I had all I went in with; diary, bag, coat etcetera., I got in the car and switched on the ignition, ready to drive off. It was then that I noticed a squeak coming from the front of the car and cursed, thinking something mechanical had gone wrong. I turned the engine off and then on again. Another squeak! Then the squeak changed to a muted, "M e o w w w!"

I instantly knew what had happened, and realised that Mrs Miggins had climbed in my bag while we were in the other room.

I returned to the house without opening the bag. I stepped through the door and went straight in, shouting, "It's only the nurse!"

The young man came towards me. "I can't find Mrs Miggins."

I returned the concern with a big grin. I placed my bag on

the floor and out popped a little kitten. We both laughed and I was pleased to see the two reunited. Needless to say, I then drove to the surgery where I replaced all of my sterile equipment to prevent cross infection.

Don't Sit Down!

Bath assessments were quite a common referral, made by hospitals or any other concerned party. The time of year was late November, not my favourite season. The clocks had gone back; the days were cold and the weather damp and dismal. I had been asked to see a gentleman who had been in hospital for some weeks. He needed an assessment to check if he could manage to bathe himself.

The house was in a built-up area, and the locality could be a bit rough. I knocked on the door but no one came to answer it. After a few tries at making the man hear me, I pushed open the door and shouted my usual, "It's only the nurse!"

Having heard me enter, the man directed me by his voice to where he was. He lived in what would be described as a bedsit. As I entered the room, he was laid on top of his bed, fully dressed.

I explained why I had come and that I would be asking some questions. I would then assess if he could manage bathing, or if he needed help in any other way. Possibly, physical help may be needed from the auxiliary nurse, better known as the 'bath nurse'.

His single bed was next to the wall and there was a small table which he used as a bedside cabinet. This held his drinks, clock and whatever else he may have needed. He was about to get up. This was ideal, as I could see how he managed getting in and out of bed. At the other end of the bed was a chair with a tea towel on it and near the window was a big armchair, which I assumed he would aim for when he got up.

I suggested he make his way to the big chair, and I would sit on the stand chair with the tea towel on. Immediately he froze.

"DURRN SIT THEER!" he yelled at me.

I was quite taken aback by the ferocity of his words. I didn't sit down, but asked why on earth I wasn't allowed to do so, as I had notes to write and found this difficult to do in a standing position. He repeated, "Tha carn'd sit theer – thar's a gun under t'cloth."

I stood very still and looked at him to try to see if he was mentally 'all there'. I carried on with the conversation and decided to humour him. "Well, if there's a gun under there, it's not going to be loaded!"

He looked up at me and said quietly, "Well, it's no bloody good if it ain't! Thar's nowt surer n'that!" At that point, I realised he was not joking.

My mind was running riot and I was trying (but probably failing) to wear my NFE. At this point, I was riveted to the ground. I could see from some photos that he was a World War II veteran. Despite this, at seventy-six, he would not be as good at handling a gun as he was in 1939.

He went on to say, "thar's bin loads o' folk robb'd 'rhand 'ere, an' I ain't gonna be one on em'!"

At this point, I fully believed that the gun would be used if he felt the need.

It was time for me to get out of there… rapidly. I think I said something about having (yet another) meeting to go to, and that I would have to leave, but would come back later. (Hell would freeze over first.) With only half a NFE, I returned to my car and escaped. I felt with this situation, patient confidentiality was insignificant and I related the whole experience to my boss. She reported the incident to the police. Tea towels no longer held the same meaning for me after that.

Widescreen Telly

Back on the district, I was out and about on my round of visits. I called at many houses and each was unique. When new patients came into our care, the assessing nurse would make note of any useful information which would enable us to plan the workload, such as hazard warnings or information useful to visiting medics. A prime example was the cleanliness of the homes we went to. This may sound critical, but it was more to do with health and safety risks.

One such house seemed to be lacking in the idea of simple cleanliness and it was necessary to take a newspaper to sit on. Firstly, we needed to remove any unnecessary outer clothing and leave it in the car. This particular house was the home to a couple of dogs and a cat. There was also a large widescreen television, a rarity in those days. It must have cost a fortune at the time. It was the only item of furniture to receive any tender loving care.

I entered warily as I had been warned about the state of the house. It had not seen a vacuum cleaner, duster or anything else associated with cleaning for quite some time. The television was the main focal point; the grown-ups and the kids crowded around it proudly. I had been warned to step carefully when I entered and, sure enough, I just missed the first pile of dog excrement at the entrance. I held my newspaper, wondering where I would be invited to sit. I furtively looked around, and saw an unused chair (not used because it wasn't in sight of the big screen).

I moved towards it and gingerly put down the newspaper. As I glanced around, there was more animal excrement in the living room, along with something I think the cat had regurgitated. The smell was overwhelming. I glanced at Mum and then at the kids. They seemed not to notice, so intent were they on watching the large screen. I managed to find the nursing notes and made the decision not to revisit this household.

Tactfully, I suggested that the treatment room in the surgery would be a good option. Mum's leg ulcer was improving and a visit to the surgery would mean she knew exactly what time she would be attending so she could plan her television viewing around it. That seemed to work. A brilliant idea; for the first time, she actually looked at me instead of at the telly. I couldn't bring myself to open my nursing bag in that environment, so suggested that there was no time like the present to make these arrangements. She could come to the treatment room the very next day. Success!

It must have been a satisfactory outcome because I was offered a cup of tea. I lied, saying that I'd just been given one at the previous house, but thanked her very much. At that point, I made my retreat but was very careful where I placed my feet on my way out. I believe I left the newspaper behind in my rush to leave.

Little Lodgers

Thankfully, most homes were pretty well kept and only few were somewhat lacking in cleanliness. I had been given a new referral via the hospital, to visit a lady who had undergone surgery to her leg. It seemed pretty routine and I was to check if she needed a regular visit or if she just needed advice and could visit the treatment room. I knocked on the door, and shouted my usual, "It's only the nurse."

I was invited in, as long as I was quick to enter and I immediately closed the door.

It became apparent that the need for speed was due to the number of dogs present in the house. I think I counted seven of them. Mother had six puppies, who were just finding their feet (or should I say paws?). I have to say that they were absolutely gorgeous, but were jumping and playing everywhere.

I explained to the lady that I wanted to see her wound and redress it afterwards. I could then make a decision as to whether the treatment room was appropriate.

The puppies were fussing and sniffing at me so I requested that just until we had sorted out her dressings, perhaps they could be shut in another room? They were duly removed and I could get on with the task in hand. After the usual hand washing, I began to lay out the sterile field on the table, whilst the lady positioned herself to have the old dressing removed. Everything was going well until I was about to put on the new dressing.

Then 'it' appeared.

At first I wasn't sure, it was walking along the tablecloth. Then it jumped. OMG! A flea. Another, and then another. They were marching into battle.

Just as I was placing the dressing on the wound, the leader of the pack jumped onto her leg at exactly the same time. I'd just pinioned the flea neatly onto the wound. I was in quandary, if I lifted up the dressing, would the rest of the team join the leader?

I looked at my patient, she looked at me, and we both looked at her leg. There was nowhere in the house that the dogs had not been, so it was logical that there would be little armies of fleas everywhere.

It was decision time; do I re-dress or not re-dress? No one told me about this when I was doing my training. Eventually, we agreed that she would attend the treatment room that afternoon and I would make a point of being there to do the dressing myself.

Many animals have fleas and I did sympathise with the patient, who had been in hospital overnight whilst a friend babysat the dogs. She was mortified at the number of 'lodgers' that had appeared. I believe the problem was resolved within a couple of days but she continued to attend the treatment room, just in case.

A BIT EXTRA ON THE AGENCY

Not Easy Peasy

During the latter days of my district nursing escapades, I was beginning to feel the need to stay in one place, that is to go to a warm nursing home or hospital, and stay there for the full duration of my shift. I decided to try a few shifts doing agency work, with a view to checking out the nursing homes as part of my research. I knew there would be the odd home visit, but this involved doing a full eight to twelve hour shift rather than a multitude of visits like we did on the district.

On one of my more memorable agency shifts, I looked after an elderly lady at her home. The house was in a very rural area on the outskirts of Bolton. Fields surrounded the property and the cottage was only accessible via a meandering dirt track. The little lady, whom I shall call Rose, was a very petite, frail little soul. Her son lived quite close by and was a local farmer. By the time I arrived at 9 p.m. she was already in bed in the front room, which looked out over the fields of her son's farmland.

The cottage had not been modernised and had stone floors, a coal fire and a recently-installed indoor toilet. The outdoor one still existed but Rose was no longer able to get to it. Even with the indoor loo, she needed a commode next to her bed at night.

There were hens everywhere and they were definitely free range; there seemed to be scores of them when I arrived for my first night shift. Her son had detailed all the nursing requirements for his mother to the agency. I was then given the information I needed, but not in its entirety as I was to learn later.

It was a warm and balmy night in late summer when I first met Rose. The door key was where I had been told it had been hidden. I was to attend to her toilet needs, make her drinks, give her medication as required and generally make her comfortable for the night. As I looked around at the views and isolated farms dotted around, I began to think this was going to be quite a pleasant job.

Even though it was summer, the fire was burning in the hearth, supplying hot water to make life a little easier for washing and hygiene purposes. The coal bucket had been replenished for the night and my main task were to keep Rose peaceful and happy.

After parking my car I walked towards the back door, by-passing the dozen or so hens as they ambled about on the little piece of land outside. I let myself in and found Rose in her bed, looking out towards the fields. There was no need for closed curtains as nothing and no-one overlooked the little cottage.

I looked into the converted front room, and found Rose semi-sleeping and expecting my visit for the night. I made sure she heard my voice so she would not be startled. Her double bed was covered with an eiderdown, something that nowadays has been replaced by the duvets which are lighter and warmer.

I had been told that she enjoyed a cup of warm milk with a drop of sherry in it, just before going to sleep. Of course, this would be one of my first tasks, to help her have a good night's sleep. She was wearing a cotton bonnet, very much like the ones seen in Victorian times and I felt I had been transported into a different century. She whispered to me that she would like her warm milk after I had rounded up the hens, and got them safely in the hut.

"PARDON?"

She repeated the instructions quite clearly. "You need to get the 'ens in, or t'fox'll get 'em!" Loosely translated: the hens need to be in the shed, as there are a few foxes about that will attack them. I gathered that this little bit was some of the 'missing information'.

So it was I found myself outside trying to chivvy the hens into going to the shed for the night. I am not sure how it came about but eventually they made their way into the hut and I could shut the door, knowing that none would become breakfast for the local foxes.

I returned to Rose, with some pride, and informed her that her hens were safe. The next task was to make her milk and sherry. This proved to be a little more difficult than expected. It seemed that the kettle was in the hearth for a reason, along with a heavy metal pan that had burn marks on its base.

This was my next challenge; the milk was to be warmed up on the fire, because the wood burning cooker was not lit for evening use. I found the milk in the pantry and proceeded to pour it into the pan, which I then placed onto the embers of the fire. (I had vague memories of this from my childhood, when coal fires were common.)

I must say that toast and other such things did have a better taste than when cooked in modern day toasters. I had forgotten about how long it took to warm things, so I was on hold watching the milk in the pan. Eventually, lovely warm milk landed in Rose's mug, along with a tot of sherry to help her sleep.

I proudly took her the mixture and she sipped at it, and then spat some out! I must have done something wrong, but what? I was soon to find out as she said to me, "Did you put any sherry in? I can't taste it!"

At this point, I took the mug and emptied some of the liquid out, and added more sherry, returning with the drink to get her approval.

"Thowt yer worr gonna put sum'more sherry in?"

By this time, I believe a third of the mug was sherry and the other two thirds warm milk. Off I went again, re-warmed the drink and added more sherry – about half and half by this time. She took another sip. I waited with bated breath for the satisfied smile, but she said, "Yer needs to lift yer elbow up a bit more."

I didn't need to ask what she meant by that.

Back in the kitchen, and another re-warming of the milk, but this time it was two thirds sherry and a third milk. I proffered the mug to Rose and she took a gulp from it. This time no words were needed, I saw a smile start to spread on her face, and heard the "Aaaahh!" of a satisfied customer.

I made note for any future staff, of Rose's preferences in the warm milk department – and the round-up of hens.

During my time spent at the cottage, I was never really alone. The hen food was kept in the pantry store, which then became a fast food restaurant for various little critters – mainly mice! This seemed to be part and parcel of life in the countryside.

I grew quite fond of Rose over time. Things were pretty routine once I got used to the hens and coal fire, had perfected my warm milk and given names to the mice. Even the hens seemed to recognise me.

A few weeks later, I arrived to find that the key was not where it should have been.

I decided to see if Rose was in her usual place in bed in the front room. I found my way to the window where she would look out from her bed, to see if she was okay. I could definitely see her chest rising and falling. Her cotton bonnet was a little skewed to one side, so I tapped gently on the window. No response. I banged louder. Still no response. I tried to raise the sash window, but was unable to lift it. After a few minutes, I knew I would have to contact the relatives via the care agency I worked for. Eventually, they told me that Rose's son was on his way over the field to try and gain entry. He arrived a few minutes later, and sure enough, she had left the key in the lock and rendered the door useless unless it was broken down.

Rose's son went to the front room window and began to jiggle it until it eventually opened and he could climb through. Rose remained oblivious to this. As her son opened the back door for me, I could hear the loud sound of snoring coming from the front room. He looked at me, and grinning widely. "She's drunk as a skunk – bin at the sherry agen. Ah'll geet them 'ens in whil' ahm 'ere."

Again translated this meant that he would round up the

hens and put them in the shed for the night. Rose had been a bit generous earlier with the sherry bottle, but at age ninety-one, who on earth would be bothered?

Seasonal Wishes

Nursing homes are usually short of staff over Christmas and New Year and, not having any commitments at home, I was happy to work any shifts over the holiday period, along with the extra pay that went with it. I had done a few shifts at a nursing home in Bacup and the owners and regular staff knew me well. I was happy to fill the gaps when no trained staff were available. The evening shift was usually around 1p.m. until 9.30 p.m. The last fifteen minutes were used to give hand-over information to the night staff.

It had been a pleasant Christmas Eve and, besides the usual nursing care, we were busy wrapping parcels and preparing for the next day. Christmas Day was given to making it as special as possible for the patients, who perhaps didn't have anyone in their lives. I was updating the notes ready to hand over to the night staff when the telephone rang. I answered in my usual way, giving the name of the home and my nursing title.

There was silence at the other end, so I repeated what I had just said. Then I heard someone (a male) say, "Don't put the phone down," which, of course, I wasn't in the habit of doing during any conversations. He seemed to stutter a little. "D-d-don't p-p-put the phone down will you?" Again, I reassured the man that I wouldn't do that.

Then came the question. "A-r-r-re you wearing b-b-black stockings?"

Now I began to understand. The opportunist on the other end was about to do his bit as a heavy breather.

In answer to his question, I said, "It's cold out there, and I am wearing thick woolly tights." Then, came the next question.

"A-r-r-re you w-w wearing panties? D-d-d-don't put the phone d-d-down!"

"Of course!" I replied. "At this time of year, I always wear nice thick ones to keep me warm!"

Next came the heavy breathing, very laboured, and I had the impression he was doing other things in the phone box.

"You don't sound very well," I responded, "Do you need a doctor?"

"No," he replied, "I n-n-need you!"

On the spur of the moment, I decided I would settle this once and for all. "Look," I said, "I finish my shift in fifteen minutes. If I give you directions, you could meet me afterwards? How does that sound?"

SILENCE.

The laboured breathing stopped; no background activity, just silence.

I was about to ask his name, but by this time, the phone had gone dead. Oh well! I never did get my blind date; I can only assume that his Christmas Eve was spent phoning other nurses and hoping for a better response than the one I gave.

Time to Go

Life as a district nurse was varied and sometimes arduous. Many times the visits were difficult but I became fond of my patients. I was treated as a friend and confidante. It was emotionally fraught at times, we gave care to the terminally ill, and we sometimes became the families' lifeline. Over the thirty years I nursed, things changed and evolved. My job was becoming more managerial due to an increasing amount of information having to be documented. It felt like I had moved away from the hands on nursing which I had always loved. It was time for me to move on and discover other ways of caring for people. I found this by venturing into an area that was different and challenging. I took on the job of what is commonly known as a mobile warden. Simultaneously, I trained as a call centre operator, dealing with alarm calls from both sheltered housing schemes and private properties.

Again, I wanted to pick out only the funnier side of life associated with this. The sad and heartfelt calls, I will leave to others. Dealing with human tragedy and illness affected me greatly, and I know I did my very best for these people. However, the funny side of life is what brings cheer and laughter, and hopefully my stories reflect this.

PART TWO

2007
A New Job

The organisation I joined had recently changed hands and had expanded. The company building was an old mill converted into offices and, being a listed building, looked and felt to have character.

Three of us were in a team and each of us was on call for seventy-two hours, then had six days off. This was known as a rolling rota. As a mobile responder, we worked alone and, when the scheme managers in sheltered housing were off duty or on holiday, we dealt with any urgent calls. The clients would pull their emergency cords, and we would go out to them and organise any help which was needed. For obvious reasons, the bulk of our work tended to be outside of office hours.

The call centre would phone up and inform us of the problem the client was having. In many instances, the clients may have pressed their emergency buttons accidentally and often didn't realise they had done so until I or a colleague had arrived at their door. Despite the call centre trying to speak to the client, it sometimes was not heard or was ignored. So this type of call was named a 'no reply call', which would need investigating. We also attended clients who needed hospital attention, giving access to the ambulance crew or even the police and the fire brigade.

Call the Fire Brigade

Many of the fire alarm call-outs were false alarms, but we needed to attend to ensure the safety of all concerned. Meal times were a common time to get this type of call. Burnt meals were a frequent cause of the alarm going off. However, one call came through to me at around eleven thirty at night, and very few would be cooking at that time. I hurriedly got dressed and made my way to the sheltered housing scheme where the alarm had been sounding. I knew I couldn't make it before the fire crew as the station was right next door to the scheme. I believe some of the residents found it of great interest to watch the fire crews speed into action, getting dressed and into the fire engine in a very rapid time.

I arrived at the scheme to the smell of smoke and of something smouldering. It was most unusual to have a real fire. When the crew declared it was safe to enter the flat, following the extinguishing of flames inside, I glanced towards the resident who was looking shaken but also quite sheepish.

The chief fire officer was holding something by his gloved fingertips and declared he had found the offending item which had caused the fire. There was a bit of a wry grin on the officers' faces, so I took a closer look. As I examined this very black and charred object, I felt puzzled. This burnt offering wasn't food, but a fur covered pencil case with a metal zip. I looked questioningly at the lady who owned this article.

"Well I was cold; I thought it would be okay," she said.

On her now unoccupied bed, was a microwaveable wheat bottle, which she used almost every night.

She said the wheat bottle worked very well, but needed another to warm her hands up. It seems that, in her inventive way, she had decided to use a pencil case as an alternative to another wheat bag. The effect was quite amazing; once in the microwave, it sounded like explosives going off. Not only was it quite noisy, but the accompanying smoke and burning was even more alarming.

And of course, the fire alarm initiated a chain reaction; the attendance of a full fire crew in her living room, relatives, the mobile responder, and all the other tenants following the fire drill. The poor woman was mortified and very apologetic. Once everything was safe, the fire crew left and I did my best to console her. She didn't need to be told to keep metal objects out of the microwave; she had learned this lesson very quickly. It was suggested that an electric blanket was more suitable for keeping warm.

Knock Knock – who's there?

Not all sheltered housing is within one building. Many bungalows and houses were built where the more independent folk could live peacefully, but could still have the security of the lifelines and various other facilities.

I received a no reply call from one such residence and went to investigate why the emergency pull cord had been used. Unlike with the sheltered schemes, there was no way I could enter one of these buildings. I knocked and knocked and pressed the doorbell but there was no response. In cases like this, we needed to call the police to break in. The call centre requested their presence and within minutes they had arrived, much to the interest of the surrounding neighbours. After assessing the situation, and still no reply, one officer went to his van to retrieve 'the key': a battering ram used for breaking into property.

I stood back and watched the police at work. After checking with neighbours to find out if the occupant had been seen that day, the police prepared to break in. Just as they were about to do this, a car rolled up and came to a halt outside the flats. As he lowered his window, the driver became increasingly concerned. He was very aware of the commotion and increasing crowds.

"What's going on? I live here, what's happened?"

The police lowered the battering ram, and we all went to the car, explaining that his emergency lifeline had been used, and we needed to check if the occupant was OK.

As he got out of the car, he began to look a little embarrassed. He unlocked the front door and looked inside. His flat was upstairs and there, right at the top, was a black Labrador dog. The man had placed a baby gate on the landing so his dog couldn't escape down the stairs.

As we got nearer to the top step, it became very clear what had happened and Benji had tell-tale evidence hanging from his jaws. Benji had become a little bored when his owner nipped out to the shops. The orange pull cord was somewhat shorter than normal, and the remainder of it was hanging out of the dog's mouth. His tail wagged repeatedly as the four of us climbed the stairs. He was very pleased to have the company of two coppers, a mobile warden, and his owner.

Luckily for the man, the damage was minimal, but had the door been broken down, this would have been a different story.

It was nice to have a happy ending. We all went on our way wearing a little smile on our faces.

Cut Price Services

We had another client who regularly pulled his alarm cord. He was a little man who had previously suffered a stroke, which affected his speech. When he spoke to the call centre they had great difficulty understanding what he was saying. This usually meant dispatching the services of the mobile responder to check if any assistance was needed. He managed to get about with a stick, and frequently went to the pub for a bevvy or two.

My colleague had visited the previous day (a twenty-mile round trip). The man's 'emergency' turned out to be that he had run out of cigarettes and wanted her to go to the shop to get some. This, unsurprisingly, was not one of the services we offered. He was informed that we were there for genuine emergencies only and he would have to ask someone else to go to the shop.

When he pulled the alarm again I managed to arrive within my twenty minute desired response time. Once I was inside, he started to tell me that he had been robbed. This of course meant that the police had to be involved. As he began to tell his tale, it slowly dawned on me that perhaps there were other things to be taken into account regarding the 'robbery'.

As his story unravelled, it seems that he had gone to the pub earlier that evening. On this occasion, he had been approached by a not so young woman, asking if he needed her services. I enquired if he would recognise her again as he had insisted it was she who had 'robbed' him. His response was quite speedy and he could describe the more obvious features, for example, she had got a false leg. This would be quite useful for identification.

She had returned with him to his flat and provided the services she specialised in. However, it seems that at the end of the 'therapy session', he had fallen asleep on his bed. The lady of the night (or should I say 'day'?) proceeded to remove the fee from his jacket pocket.

As the discussion went on, the man seemed to retract the 'been robbed' bit, as he realised that she had merely taken her fee. In fact, he was adamant I told no-one about the incident. This of course was impossible, as I had to report back to the call centre with information about the 'robbery'. However, I gave minimal information over the intercom, until I was back in my car and could fill in the gaps.

The seventy-six year old man did not want to press charges and I can only wonder if the woman with one leg had given him cut price charges? The incident was documented and passed on to the relevant people.

No Entry

One particular night, around eleven-thirty, I received a call to attend a housing scheme in Blackburn. Our response times needed to be twenty minutes or less, which meant there was no having a wash or checking your appearance before setting off. Often, I would end up putting my uniform on over the top of my night attire, just to shave off a couple of minutes.

And so I was asked to go out to a man whose call was classed as a 'no reply'. He had pressed his pendant alarm which he wore around his neck.

On this particular night, the client was not in the building, but waiting at the entrance. He was sitting on his invalid scooter near to the door. He looked a little worse for wear, in as much that he was swaying and muttering something incoherently. I moved closer to him and immediately discovered what the problem was. Simply, he was rather inebriated and couldn't reach the door panel to scan his entry fob. He was slouched forward, and was almost asleep.

I gently touched his shoulder to let him know that I had arrived and proffered my ID. Slowly he opened his eyes and grinned at me from ear to ear. I had been told later by one of the residents that they had been watching him almost hang off his scooter and that he nearly 'did himself a mischief' trying to reach the door. They hadn't let him in simply because they didn't know what mood he was in, or if he would become aggressive because of the booze.

As it happened he was as good as gold and I was able to escort him to his room. I was about to try and help him, but he seemed perfectly adept at launching himself from the scooter (which he had driven to the side of the settee) and, with a perfect landing, lay horizontally on his makeshift bed. He then closed his eyes, and was asleep in seconds. After making sure that he and his vehicle were safe, I reported back to the call centre and left a copy of the report for the scheme manager.

The Call Centre

As I became more experienced, I began to do more shifts at the call centre. This was an extremely busy time, as this service covered much of the country – from Cumbria to

Oxford and more. The head office was, in fact, in the town where I lived. It was easy for me to come in and work some of the shifts when they were short staffed.

In the earlier days, before the client numbers grew, the night shift was quieter and we updated client details on the computer system. Because the company was spreading out, the volume of calls increased.

We're Flooding!

During one of my night shifts, a man pulled his emergency cord and was obviously quite distressed. We could check on the notes about his personal details and any other information which was relevant to him. It seemed he lived with his wife in one of the schemes in the Manchester area. As I tried to discover the problem, he repeatedly said that water was coming in and it was flooding his lounge. If I were to call the emergency services, I needed to know where the water was coming in. Asking this question repeatedly did not get me anywhere.

"Sir, I need to know where the water is coming from, so I can call either a plumber or the fire brigade!"

He replied, "Oh! It's getting deeper!"

"SIR, WHERE IS THE WATER COMING FROM?"

"It's up to her knees!"

"SIR, WHERE IS THE WATER COMING FROM?"

"OOOOH! SHE'S FLOATING, SHE'S FLOATING!"

"That'll be the fire brigade then, sending for them now…"

I called the fire brigade, the mobile warden, and the relatives, staying on the line with the client whose wife was now 'floating'. On arrival, the fire officer came through to say that they had checked the source of the leak; it was coming from the bathroom sink tap. Indeed there was water everywhere, but only around three centimetres or so. It appeared that the occupant of the flat underneath, was the one in more danger. The water had dripped through to the electrics, and this had to be isolated and the occupants moved to another flat.

After the initial help from the fire brigade, the relatives set to, trying to soak up as much of the water as possible. It was all sorted out in the end, but a vision of 'the wife' floating around in her chair was etched in my memory forever.

Reading in the Car

The call centre work was varied and busy, and there were many policies and procedures in place. The decisions were mostly in the hands of the operator. Because I did both jobs – mobile and operator – it was common to have to call out one of my own team. On one occasion, a resident in the area my team covered pulled the cord to express some deep concerns about a strange car parked outside. She commented that the driver looked a bit suspicious. However, I needed to know if his actions were suspicious and if the police needed to be involved along with the mobile warden.

On further questioning, the woman said that he'd 'been doing things in his car'. Asking her to explain a little more, she said, "You know...D O I N G things!"

I had to answer honestly, and replied that we couldn't send anyone out unless what he was doing was illegal.

"Well, it IS illegal! He's been looking at one of those mucky magazines and he's errrm messing about with himself.

Right outside my flat as well!"

My response was to say that she should stay in her flat, and we would send someone along to investigate and also inform the police.

"Yes, yes," she said. "I used my binoculars, he's been there fiddling in his trousers for half an hour!"

I reassured her that someone was on their way, and made a note that she had obviously been watching his activities for quite some time before pulling her cord. The binoculars helped a great deal in the identification of the magazine. And whatever else she wished to observe.

My next task, after informing the police, was to summon my colleague to attend the scheme and document the incident. Tommy was in his early seventies, but was very fit and active. When I relayed the situation to him and asked him to attend the scheme, he truly thought I was playing a joke on him. It took some honest persuasion to convince him otherwise.

By the time the police and mobile warden arrived, the man had completed the task in hand (so to speak), and driven off. Amazingly the client, who obviously had an eye for detail, had no idea of the number plate or description of the car.

I have an Indoor Garden

It is sometimes assumed that older people are gentle and benevolent, innocent and honest. Over the years, I have found this not to be entirely true.

On one particular occasion, it was worrying that we couldn't make contact with the client. On investigation, she had left a chip pan on the cooker and gone to the shop, forgetting all about it. The fire brigade and mobile warden were on route. The relatives had also been informed.

After all parties had been informed of the situation, one of the relatives made a very pleading phone call to the centre. He promised that whatever was wrong at the flat, he and his brother would put the fire out. I reassured them that the emergency services were there to make sure everyone in the scheme was safe, and that under no circumstances would they be cancelled.

There seemed to be a groan in the background, but I assumed it was concern and apprehension regarding the fire. Indeed this turned out to be so.

They became very distressed, which of course was understandable. Since there was no reply from their mother, we were all quite anxious.

We usually kept the calls 'open' so that we could continue to communicate with the fire crew and hopefully the tenant. By this time, the relatives were on the scene, but had to wait in a safe area until the fire crew had assessed the situation. Luckily, they were in time to prevent a full blown fire in the kitchen and managed to make the scene safe.

It became embarrassingly clear why the relatives were at their wits end. We spoke to the chief fire officer, who informed us that there appeared to be a cannabis farm in the lady's bedroom. She had been sleeping on the sofa, whilst the plants were grown and cultivated in her bedroom. I'm sure that the findings became quite the topic of conversation by everyone who lived or worked in that property.

A few weeks later, a routine call came through from the same scheme.

Afterwards, I decided to check on any further information

about the lady with the chip pan fire. She had returned from the shop to find police, fire crew and mobile warden all waiting to speak to her and her sons. After a full investigation, she was evicted and had to seek accommodation elsewhere.

Good Tidings

The call centre was very active and during unsocial hours when there were no scheme managers on duty, we were extremely busy.

Each operator had their own email inbox which was checked on arrival at work. Various updates and information was also passed to us by this means.

Since we were based at the head office, the managing director and administration staff all inhabited the same building.

Early in December one year we all received a request to think about donating something towards Christmas presents for the bosses. I felt quite strongly that it should have been the workers who received a little extra. I told my supervisor, by email, that perhaps if we were paid a little more, we could afford to donate towards a gift for the bosses and, on this occasion, I would decline the invite. I'm sure I added a few more words in a similar vein. Not thinking anything else about it, I carried on doing the work on the call centre.

I logged on to my shift again about a week later. As usual I checked my email for updates. I was quite taken aback; there were scores of emails in my inbox, when there were usually no more than half a dozen. They were coming from people who worked in Cumbria, Yorkshire, Manchester, Oxford and virtually every area that was covered by the centre. I began opening them, to find that I had got a retinue of followers. Many had written about how pleased they were, that someone had stuck up for the workers and they agreed whole heartedly with what I had said. For quite some time, I was confused. How did they know about my comments? I was sure I hadn't told anyone except my supervisor exactly what I thought.

Very early in my shift, I was summoned to the office, to discuss the email.

That day, I learned a lot more about writing emails.

I thought I had responded privately to my supervisor, giving my views about collecting for the bosses' Christmas gifts.

NOT SO.

In my haste to clarify my thoughts on the matter, I had clicked on 'reply all' instead of 'reply'. Now this didn't mean anything to me but, after a swift explanation by my senior, I learned rapidly what 'reply all' meant.

It seems that my email was sent to every member of staff up and down the country, including the managing director and other senior staff. I must say I was mortified. To this day, I am very wary of clicking on 'reply all'.

It took some time for the waters to settle, but I also made some new email buddies, and lots of admirers.

That's 'a Fail'

I quite enjoyed doing the night shift at the call centre. We knew that the out of hours calls from schemes meant that we were ensuring, as far as possible, the safety of the people who lived there.

It was one summer, in the late evening, when an

emergency pull cord was used. Most of the tenants knew the identity of their peer groups who lived within the scheme. On this occasion, it appeared that there was a stranger in their midst.

Prostrate on the floor was a man who could not be identified by any of the tenants. He was sleeping soundly, and no one really wanted to waken him. This was definitely a job for the mobile warden, who was quickly contacted. When the warden got back to us, it seemed no one knew the man, or how he managed to enter the building because he would have needed a key or code to gain access.

The man was duly roused by the mobile warden, and appeared to be 'worse for wear', in as much that he was quite drunk and a little incoherent. Eventually, he was asked where he lived.

"Here," was his reply.

When he was told the name and address of the scheme, he looked a little puzzled. "No, I don't live at that address," he said, confused.

Finally, the mobile responder managed to get him to give his name and address. He was about eighty years old and, apart from the unsteadiness caused by the booze, he seemed fairly fit. It appeared that he made his way from the pub to what he thought was home. Some kind soul, who had just moved into the scheme and didn't know the residents, had let him in when they had returned.

Once we could match him to the correct address, the warden ended up putting him in his car and taking him there. This was not really allowed, but just on this occasion the rules became a little bendy.

Perhaps in future, a taxi would be more appropriate.

STILL A JOKER

April Fool

I hope I have shown I have still retained a sense of humour, which recently had the chance to expand on a visit to my dentist. I have my normal six-monthly check-ups and go through the routine like most other people.

For some reason, I felt the urge to play a little trick on my male dentist. It was the beginning of April and I felt it was appropriate to create a small diversion for him. I have never been one to worry about or detest my dental visits, so I decided to have a little fun. My dentist at the time was not famous for his customer interaction. I knew that his usual question at check-ups would be, "Have you any problems at the moment?"

Armed with this knowledge, I purchased a set of toy vampire teeth, with nicely elongated front fangs. When my turn came, the usual, "Any problems?" was uttered, to which I answered, "Well yes, actually I do".

I turned to sit on the chair, my back was facing the dentist, and as I swung around, I placed the fangs in my mouth.

I answered the question by telling him that my front teeth

seemed to be growing. To prove the point I gave him a big smile. Just for a moment, he didn't seem able to work out what he was seeing. However, the dental nurse was in front of me when I put in the fangs. By this time, she had tears streaming down her face, and was laughing uncontrollably (she hadn't heard of the NFE).

The dentist focused on my tooth arrangement with puzzlement. Then it dawned on him; the fangs were a new addition to my mouth. Eventually, he managed to get some words out regarding my April Fools' prank.

"Oh! How funny!" was his response.

I believe that this little diversion was the focus of conversation when the staff took their breaks. I thought it would lighten the load a little.

On that note, I shall rest my pen.

Not the End

I was diagnosed with inoperable Lung Cancer in 2013. I had expected to live for only about six months. I have no idea why I have survived but I am still here, and indeed, live to tell the tale!